Dedication
Dedicated to the
Mother herself whose life
continues to be a source of inspiration

Acknowledgements

I am grateful to God for providing me the inspiration and opportunity to write this biography of a great saint. Special thanks to my children for understanding and cooperating with me and putting up with inconveniences while I wrote this book. I would also like to thank the publisher for choosing to publish this biography.

Publisher's Note

One of the best ways to understand the complex human nature and the world is through reading biographies. Biographies of different personalities can help us understand what are the different aspects of things which make or break a person. What are the issues which cause war and what are the aspects which bring peace in human life. What is something a person earns for and what is something which can make a person change his entire perspective. What are those life turning incidences which affect human mind and psychology. The lives of the successful can teach you how to go about enriching your life and creating your own future. You can learn from their mistakes and victories.

People are always interested to read about people who inspire them. But there are many facts which remain hidden from the general public. The idea of bringing this series of biographies is to bring out those facts which have till date not been made public or made available at one platform. The author Mamta Sharma Ghuge has done extensive research to explore the inside out of the person's life who is being written about and has brought out many facts which remained hidden before.

We hope you like this series of books and would be happy to get a feedback from you.

Kuldeep Jain

C.E.O., B. Jain Publishers (P) Ltd.

Contents

Chapter 1

Introduction

'Our aim is to quench the infinite thirst of Jesus Christ for love by the profession of the evangelical counsels and by whole-hearted free service to the poorest of the poor, according to the teaching and the life of our Lord in the gospel, revealing in a unique way, the salvation of God... Our particular mission is to labor at the salvation and sanctification of the poorest of the poor...we are called the Missionaries of Charity.'

Embodiment of love, kindness and selfless service, Mother Teresa spent her life tending to the poor, sick and the abandoned. To those who were left on the streets to die while the world watched in silence and indifference, she became the caregiver. What the world witnessed was a divine being, full of compassion, doing God's will on earth. Believing that there is God in every human being, she said, "I see God in every human being. When I wash the leper's wounds, I feel I am nursing the Lord himself. Is it not a beautiful experience?" Mother Teresa maintained that it is preferable to make mistakes in kindness than work miracles in unkindness.

An inspiring life full of courage, endurance, devotion to the service of God and humanity, the greatness of her deeds and the meaningful life that she lived will continue to be there in the hearts of the people she served. For her:

'Life is an opportunity, benefit from it. Life is beauty, admire it. Life is bliss, taste it. Life is a dream, realize it. Life is a challenge, meet it. Life is a duty, complete it. Life is a game, play it. Life is a promise, fulfill it. Life is sorrow, overcome it. Life is a song, sing it. Life is a struggle, accept it. Life is a tragedy, confront it. Life is an adventure, dare it. Life is luck, make it. Life is too precious, do not destroy it. Life is life, fight for it.'

There is poverty, suffering and deprivation all around us. We continue to carry on with our lives, unfazed by the plight of homeless families and starving children around us. It is important to awaken our inner self and extend a helping hand. Mother Teresa endlessly worked for the needy and the downtrodden. Her efforts did not go in vain. The Missionaries of Charity founded by her as a small organization with thirteen members in Calcutta has a visible and active presence all over the world today.

Considered by the world as a saint, she was a committed voice of love and faith. The pain, loneliness – we all undergo this at some point or the other in our lives – everyone pines for love. Faith was of utmost importance to her. Give yourself to God and he will do great things through you. 'The more you have, the more you are occupied, less you give. Poverty is not mortification but penance.' Mother Teresa continued to pray and urge everyone to understand the words of Jesus: 'Love one another as I have loved you.' When a poor person dies of disease or hunger, it is not that God did not want to take care of that person but because we were not willing to give what was needed. These needs can be material or emotional. She once narrated an incident when she picked up a woman from a garbage dump. The woman was on the verge of dying but what was troubling her was not the fear of death but the fact that her son had abandoned her. Mother Teresa urged her to forgive her son which the woman eventually did after a long time. 'If we really want to love, we must learn how to forgive.' There is only one God and He is for all. Therefore, everyone must be treated equally, without discrimination on either religious or economic grounds.

Disruption of peace in today's world begins at home. There is a mad rush for material acquisitions; children do not have time for their parents, in fact parents themselves have very little time for each other. Constant ambition for fast growth and efforts to satisfy unlimited wants is desensitizing us towards humanitarian causes. Unless we decide to inculcate love for the masses, we will be killing ourselves with work and 'work without love is slavery.'

'We can do no great things, only small things with great love. God cannot be found in noise and restlessness. God is the friend of silence. See how nature – trees, flowers, grass, etc. grow in silence. See the stars, the moon, the sun, how they move in silence. The more we receive in silent prayer, the more we can give in our active life.'

For Mother Teresa, service to humanity came first and foremost. It was important to love the poor, serve them. The confidence that God does not put more burdens on a person than what he/ she can carry, she relentlessly worked for the downtrodden. Peace in the world and within is lacking because we have forgotten that we belong to each other. What matters is not how much one does but how much love goes into that act. She voiced her opinions very clearly on issues like abortions, peace, poverty, love and service to humanity. If it is not feasible for one person to feed a hundred people, then just feed one. With love it is possible to touch the souls of people – there is more hunger for love in this world than food. Her stand on abortion remains controversial till date. She opposed the practice openly saying that how can we say there are many children? It is like saying there are many flowers.

Little is known about the spiritual highs or lows of a saint who has become an icon of love and compassion for the world irrespective of their faith. The feeling of compliance with God's will and a deep sense of self-sacrifice were the motivating factors. Mother Teresa believed that love and faith go together – 'Faith is a gift of God. Without it there would be no life. And our work, to be fruitful and to be all for God, and beautiful, has to be built on faith.' Simple human thoughtfulness is the prerequisite to holiness. For her, Jesus only did good wherever he went and we should be like him. From peace making dialogues to praying for a dying child, she completely occupied herself with doing good to humanity. The writing on the wall in Mother Teresa's home for children in Calcutta read:

The good you do today, will often be forgotten.
Do good anyway.
Give the best you have, and it will never be enough.
Give your best anyway.
In the final analysis, it is between you and God.
It was never between you and them anyway.

Praying everyday was not just a ritual but a motivating factor for her. 'Dear Jesus, Help me to spread Thy fragrance everywhere I go....Stay with me and then I shall begin to shine as you shine, so to shine as to be a light to others' (from the video *Everyone, Everywhere*). The advice that was given was, each one should feel the need for prayer during the day and take the trouble to pray. If we pray we will believe, if we believe, we will love, if we love, we will serve. Prayer has the power to extend and open the heart to contain God Himself. Faith and prayer connected her with God and when these two are there, there is service. Love and faith cannot remain by themselves unless they are put in action and that is service. Mother Teresa is considered world's greatest and most honored humanitarian today. The Dalai Lama, Tibetan spiritual leader, in appreciation of her contribution said, "the spirit, compassion and dedication of Mother Teresa to serve the poorest of the poor would continue to lead human community".

'Mother Teresa was like a prophet crying in the wilderness, revealing at once my poverty, my wretchedness and my possibilities' (Mary Poplin in *Finding Calcutta*). Abraham Heschel believed that true prophets of God 'ceaselessly shatter indifference' and that was Mother Teresa's life. By serving the poor and living among them, she simultaneously shattered our indifference to God and humanity. The greatest obstacle to their work, Mother Teresa believed, comes from the fact that we are not able to spread the full love of Christ because of our human follies. Secular philosophy may fail to understand her life and her work – Mother Teresa maintained that her work was not social work but religious work.

The path to holiness is ridden with struggles, persecutions and endless sacrifices. Mother Teresa, like other saints, lived according to 'laws set for us by God'. Her life was not like a celebrities' life. It was a life lived on different principles – devotion and a sense of calling. Most of her biographies are completely reverential. The cult of celebrity will probably fail to explain the hold she continues to exercise on the conscience of the world even today. Mother Teresa neither sought nor expected any recognition; her missionary work was larger than life. This biography is a humble attempt to get to know Mother Teresa, whose radiance lit the world and draw inspiration from her life. As we traverse this journey together, let us hope that we will be dragged out of the darkness of ignorance and indifference into a bright world with peace, love, sharing and happiness.

Chapter 2
Fact File

Nobel peace laureate Mother Teresa, is also known as 'the Saint of the Gutters' for her work amongst the poor, dying and destitute in India and across the world.

- ➲ Name—Agnes Gonxha Bojaxhiu
- ➲ Birth—August 26, 1910 in Skopje, Macedonia. Youngest of three siblings, two sisters and one brother.
- ➲ Decision to become a missionary—1918, at the age of eighteen years.
- ➲ Father Nicolai's demise—In 1919.
- ➲ Arrival in India—1929, begins her novitiate in Darjeeling, near the Himalayan mountains.
- ➲ First vows as a nun—On May 24, 1931; chose the name 'Teresa' after her patroness St. Thérèse of Lisieux.
- ➲ Final profession—May 24, 1937; was to be known as Mother Teresa following Loreto custom. Became Mother Superior of the school.

➲ 'Call from within'—September 10, 1946 to dedicate her life for the poorest of the poor.

➲ Beginning of missionary work—In 1948, in the city of Calcutta.

➲ Permission granted by the Vatican—October 7, 1950 to start her own order. The Missionaries of Charity was officially erected as a religious institute for the Archdiocese of Calcutta.

➲ Received Indian citizenship—December 14, 1951.

➲ First home for the dying and destitute opened in Kalighat – August 22, 1952.

➲ Moved order into Mother house on Lower Circular Road—In 1953.

➲ Opened children's home – In 1955.

➲ Began mobile 'Leprosariums'—In 1957.

➲ Bought land for leper town—In 1961.

➲ Received Indian and Philippine government awards for her work—In 1962.

➲ Vatican approved order for other countries—In 1965. First house set up in Colombia.

➲ Celebration of 25 years of Missionaries of Charity— In 1975.

➲ Received Nobel Prize for Peace in humanitarian work— December 10, 1979.

➲ Received India's highest civilian honor, the 'Jewel of India' 'Bharat Ratna'—On March 22, 1980.

➲ Hospitalized in Rome with serious heart condition—In June 1983.

➲ Resigned as Superior General of Missionaries of Charity due to failing health but re-elected—In September 1990.

➲ Successor Sister Nirmala elected Superior General—March 13, 1997.

➲ Died in Mother House at the age of 87—September 5, 1997.

➲ Given a state funeral attended by international dignitaries like then US first lady Hillary Clinton—September 13, 1997.

➲ Declared 'Blessed' by Pope John Paul II, an interim stage before being named a saint—October 19, 2003.

➲ Total awards received—124. A few of them are:

➲ Padmashree Award (from the President of India), August 1962.

➲ Pope John XXIII Peace Prize, January 1971.

➲ John F. Kennedy International Award, September 1971.

➲ Jawaharlal Nehru Award for International Understanding, November 1972.

➲ Templeton Prize for 'Progress in Religion', April 1973.

➲ Nobel Peace Prize, December 1979.

➲ Bharat Ratna (Jewel of India), March 1980.

➲ Order of Merit (from Queen Elizabeth),November 1983.

➲ Gold Medal of the Soviet Peace Committee, August 1987.

➲ United States Congressional Gold Medal, June 1997.

Chapter 3
Childhood and Early Years

Mother Teresa was born to Nicola and Drane Bojoxhiu on August 26, 1910 in the capital of Republic of Macedonia, Skopje, former Ottoman Empire. At the turn of the twentieth century, the city of Skopje was a bustling commercial center. At birth, she was named Agnes Gonxhe Bojaxhiu (*Gonxhe* meaning 'rosebud' in Albanian). Although she was born on 26 August, she continued to consider the day of her baptism, 27 August as her true birthday. Her father devoted most of his time to politics and Albanian cause. He was also a successful merchant. He spoke five languages fluently and had widely traveled across Europe, the near East and north Africa. Both her parents were Catholics and of Albanian origin. Very little is known about Mother Teresa's childhood years except from her own accounts and that of her brother.

Youngest of the three children, she received communion at the age of five years and regularly attended prayer meetings with great devotion. Her father's untimely demise pushed the family into a financial crisis, leaving her mother as the sole bread winner of the family. Agnes was, at that time, eight years old. Her mother played a very crucial role in the character building of her children. Inspired by her mother's efforts and guidance of a priest, Agnes developed the inclination to carry out missionary work. Later in life, she continued to assert that 'home is where the mother is.' Her mother's influence was substantial and some of Mother Teresa's sayings were a repetition of her spiritual directives, like 'The family that prays together, stays together.' No one ever left their home empty–handed. Her mother visited a woman who had been abandoned by her family, had become an alcoholic with sores all over her body, at least once a week to do her washing and take care of her. As recalled by Mother Teresa's brother and cousin, there was no dearth of such instances and Agnes often accompanied her mother on such visits. Her mother was forever keen on passing these virtues to her children. She told them 'when you do good, do it quietly, as if you were throwing a stone into the sea.' Drana's Christian Charity offered a powerful example, helping to mould Gonxha's spiritual life and shape her destiny.

"Mine was a happy family. I had one brother and sister, but I do not like to talk about it. It is not important now. The important thing is to follow God's way, the way he leads us to do something beautiful for Him." She continued to insist on not discussing the life she had lived and its insignificance to what she had set out to achieve.

Mother Teresa had her own personality—obedient yet independent, openly challenging some of the belief systems already prevalent in society at that time. She was a good listener but followed her conscience that sometimes contradicted with what people expected of her. Even though so much of her early life was centered around the Church, her fascination for the lives and stories of missionaries continued. The thought of becoming a nun struck her only around eighteen years of age.

She decided to become a Catholic Missionary nun and spread the message of love and humanity in the world. Joining the Irish order, Institute of the Blessed Virgin Mary in Ireland, famed for its work in the Indian subcontinent, 'The Sisters of Loreto' sent her to Calcutta to teach in St Mary's School and carry out missionary work in India. She never saw her mother or sister again. She began her career teaching history and geography with dedication. Besides being hard working, she was known for her selflessness, courage and charity. A person of profound prayer and deep love, her days at the school were full of happiness. After becoming a nun, her name was changed from Agnes to Teresa. In 1937, Sister Teresa finally vowed to become 'Spouse of Jesus for Eternity', thus becoming Mother Teresa. The name was chosen after Thérèse de Lisieux, the patron saint of missionaries. She continued to teach till she became the principal of St. Mary's School in 1944. Next destination was Darjeeling where she had to undergo treatment for tuberculosis since the disease was already diagnosed. On her way to Darjeeling, she received what was later described and referred to as 'a call from within', a Divine Dictat that directed her to serve the people in misery, the destitute and the dying and share their troubles. The Bengal famine of 1943 brought misery and death to Calcutta and the outbreak of hindu/muslim violence in August 1946 worsened the situation.

"By blood, I am Albanian. By citizenship, an Indian. By faith, I am a Catholic nun. As to my calling, I belong to the world. As to my heart, I belong entirely to the Heart of Jesus."

'He called her. "Come bare my light of love." Small in stature but firm in faith, she succumbed to His will without a second thought.' Her simplicity and dedication paved the path to do this will. Mother Teresa gave her resignation from the school and 'was to leave the convent and help the poor while living among them. It was an order. To fail would have been to break the faith.' She learnt basic medicine and started visiting slums, educating and treating people.

'The Missionaries of Charity' was started to serve the poorest of the poor and be completely dedicated to their cause. Nearly two years had passed before the permission was granted to start the organization. Finally, in August 1948, the Vatican gave her permission to leave the Sisters of Loreto and to start new work under the guidance of the Archbishop of Calcutta. Wearing her blue bordered sari, Mother Teresa walked out of the gates of the Convent of Loreto and walked into the world of the poor. Each day started in communion with Jesus and The Mother walked for the unwanted and the uncared for with a rosary in her hand—to find God and serve Him.

Chapter 4
The Missionaries of Charity

Originally labeled as the *Diocesan Congregation of the Calcutta Diocese,* the Missionaries of Charity was started by Mother Teresa in October 1950 after receiving permission from the Vatican. The mission of the organization, in her own

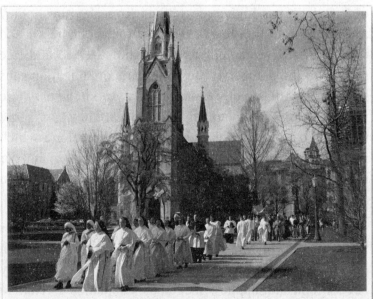

The Missionaries of Charity started by Mother Teresa at Kolkata on October 1950

words was to care for 'the hungry, the naked, the homeless, the crippled, the blind, the lepers, all those people who feel unwanted, unloved, uncared for throughout society, people that have become a burden to the society and are shunned by everyone.' Beginning as a small community with very few members in Calcutta, today it has thousands of nuns and volunteers running orphanages, centers for AIDS patients and other centers caring for refugees, the blind and the disabled, aged, alcoholics, poor and homeless, victims of floods, epidemics and famine in Asia, Africa, Latin America, North America, Australia and Europe.

The Missionaries of Charity

Missionaries of Charity is a Roman Catholic religious order which has high expectations from the nuns—they must adhere to the vows of chastity and obedience and to give their lives completely to 'wholehearted and free service to the poorest of the poor.' The organization runs schools for the street children and soup kitchens where volunteers provide the requisite services. They have more than a dozen homes in Calcutta (Kolkata) alone which include homes for women, for orphaned children and for the dying, an AIDS hospital, a school for street children and a leper colony.

Mother Teresa wrote in her diary how initial years after the setting up of Missionary of Charity were loaded with difficulties. There was no income and they had to literally beg for food and supplies. She felt the temptation to return to the comforts of the convent. There were doubts in her mind and a terrible feeling of loneliness. 'Our Lord wants me to be a free nun covered with the poverty of the cross. Today I learned a good lesson. The poverty of the poor must be so hard for them. While looking for a home I walked and walked till my arms and legs ached. I thought how much they must ache in body and soul, looking for a home, food and health. Then the comfort of Loreto (her former order) came to tempt me. 'You have only to say the word and all that will be yours again,' the tempter kept on saying... Of free choice, my God, and out of love for you, I desire to remain and do whatever be your Holy will in my regard. I did not let a single tear come.'

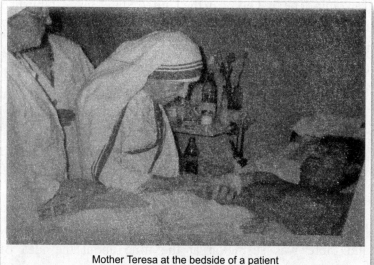

Mother Teresa at the bedside of a patient

Permission to expand the congregation was granted by Pope Paul VI with a Decree of Praise and Mother Teresa's request to spread her mission across the globe was granted.

New homes were opened all over the world; the first home was started in Venezuela, followed by others in Rome and Tanzania. The first home in the United States was established in South Bronx, New York. By 1996, she was operating 517 missions in more than 100 countries and today is assisted by over one million co-workers and billions of donations.

'Nothing to fear in God. Nothing to fear in death. God can be attained. Evil can be endured.'
—Diogenes of Oenoanda

'Situated in near segregation on the other side of the Potomac, Anacostia is the capital of Black Washington, and there was suspicion at the time about the idea of a Missionaries of Charity operation there, because the inhabitants were known to resent the suggestion that they were helpless and abject Third Worlders. Indeed, just before her press conference, Mother Teresa found her office rudely invaded by a group of black men.' (Christopher Hitchens).

The story was later narrated in great detail by her assistant Rathy Shreedhar as follows:

Mother Teresa with children

'They were very upset…They told Mother that Anacostia needed decent jobs, housing and services – not charity. Mother did not argue with them; she just listened. Finally, one of them asked her what she was going to do here. Mother said: 'First we must learn to love one another.' They did not know how to respond to that. What she hoped to accomplish was summed up as follows.

- ➲ 'The joy of loving and being loved'
- ➲ 'That takes a lot of money, doesn't it?'
- ➲ 'It takes a lot of sacrifice'
- ➲ 'Do you teach the poor to endure their lot?'

⊃ 'I think it is very beautiful for the poor to accept their lot, to share it with the passion of Christ. I think the world is being much helped by the suffering of the poor people'

Those who are believers and have faith are concerned with what we owe to God. Others who lack the initiative and willingness to do their part are relieved to see that there are some who believe. Unfortunately, the rich part of the world, barring a few exceptions, has a poor conscience.

'The scale of invocation – the world's suffering people, all God's children. What we have here is a saint in the making, whose sites and relics will one day be venerated and who is already the personal object of a following that is not much short of cultish' (Christopher Hitchens).

The Organization

The first home for the dying was opened by Mother Teresa in the city of Calcutta in 1952. With the help of state authorities, she converted an abandoned hindu temple into the Kalighat Home for the Dying. It was named the Home of the Pure Heart (Nirmal Hriday). Providing them with medical care, the Home also ensured that people who could not live with dignity get the opportunity to die with dignity. Inmates were accorded rituals in line with their religious beliefs. 'A beautiful death,' the Mother said, 'is for people who lived like animals to die like angels—loved and wanted.'

Quickly, on the heels of Nirmal Hriday, a home for those suffering from leprosy was opened and it was named Shanti Nagar (City of Peace). In addition to this, several clinics were opened throughout the city to provide medicines, food and bandages to those afflicted by this ailment. Another area of concern was increasing number of lost and homeless children. Nirmala Shishu Bhavan (Children's Home of the Immaculate Heart) was opened in 1955 to care for the orphans and homeless youth.

The Missionaries of Charity Brothers was founded in 1963, and a contemplative branch of the Sisters followed in 1976. Honoring the requests of many priests, in 1981 Mother Teresa also began the Corpus Christi Movement for Priests, and in 1984 founded with Fr. Joseph Langford the Missionaries of Charity Fathers to combine the vocational aims of the Missionaries of Charity with the resources of the ministerial priesthood. Extending her work to other countries, breaking national and regional boundaries, Mother Teresa actively involved herself in rescuing children and traveling through the war zone accompanied by the Red Cross workers and by brokering a temporary cease-fire between the Israeli army and Palestinian rebels during the Siege of Beirut. With the crumbling of Communist Bloc in eastern Europe in 1980's, she moved her operations to these countries which had previously rejected the presence of her organization. A number of projects were started in this region. No amount of criticism could deter Mother Teresa from pursuing her goals.

From assisting the hungry in Ethiopia, radiation victims at Chernobyl to helping people afflicted by natural disasters across the globe, the list was endless. By 1996, she was running 517 missions in more than 100 countries. After leaving Albania, she returned to her homeland in 1991 to start a Missionaries of Charity Brothers home in Tirana, Albania.

Statue of Mother Teresa in Prishtina, Kosovo

Acceptance by the religious community is subject to four vows that the members of the congregation are expected to take. In addition to the three basic vows of poverty, chastity and obedience, a fourth vow is required pledging service to the poor, whom Mother Teresa described as the embodiment of Christ.

'To those who say they admire my courage,
I have to tell them that I would not have any
if I were not convinced that each time
I touch the body of a leper,
a body that reeks with a foul stench,
I touch the same Christ I receive in the Eucharist'
— Mother Teresa

The Missionaries of Charity is composed of eight branches. The active and contemplative sisters have to undergo training for many years which is imparted in Calcutta, Rome, Manila, Nairobi, San Francisco and Poland. These active sisters spend the day in service of the poor and the needy while the contemplative sisters pray most of the time except for two hours in a day when they are required to serve the people. They are required to report to their regional superiors or sometimes directly to the Superior General. Active and contemplative Brothers and Missionary Fathers are also organized in a similar fashion and perform similar duties.

Being a lay missionary requires adherence to the same vows while continuing with their worldly existence. To fulfill the fourth vow of service, they can choose to be directly associated with the Missionaries of Charity or find their own Apostolate. Lay missionaries are believers but it is not a compulsion for them to stay single.

Volunteer co-workers are an integral part of the organization and share its commitment and vision. They work alongside members of the order, sacrificing their luxurious lifestyles. The Sick and Suffering Co-workers' association was formed by Jacquelinede Decker who, because of sickness and disability, was unable to join in the active work of the co-workers. Their prayers are believed to provide support and spiritual sustenance to the work of active missionaries.

To become a full fledged member takes nine years beginning with one year of familiarization. The career begins with working as assistants in Shishu Bhavan and Nirmal

Hriday. After one year, if the candidate chooses to continue, the study of scriptures, society, church history and theology marks the second phase. In the sixth year, they travel to Rome or Calcutta for a year in deep spiritual growth. In the name of personal possessions a sister is supposed to have three saries, a pair of sandals, a crucifix and a rosary. They also have a plate and metal spoon, a canvas bag, and prayer book. In cold countries, possessions also include a cardigan.

Being a volunteer is a trying yet satisfying experience. Formal permission is required to join the congregation which could take a couple of months. The waiting period often turns out to be a test of patience and commitment. Life and work at the Missionaries of Charity can be best described in the first hand accounts of volunteers. Mary Poplin, an American who enthusiastically chose to serve in Calcutta, writing in her book *'Finding Calcutta—What Mother Teresa Taught Me About Meaningful Work and Service'* said on her arrival at the Mother House:

'The Mother House was where Mother – as she is always called here – lived with a group of finally professed sisters and a larger group of novice sisters. The administrative work of the Missionaries of Charity is largely conducted here. Inside a small room off the dining area, Sister Bethany and a volunteer were speaking with newly arrived volunteers.'

'Mother Teresa often urged volunteers to come to mass and special sessions led by a priest one evening a week. After Mass, Mother Teresa often spoke with us and handed out religious medals, rosaries and especially little cards with prayers on them – Mother called them her 'business cards'. A small but constant stream of visitors appeared at the Mass and the centers.'

David Jolly, writing on Volunteering for Mother Teresa's Missionaries of Charity in *New York Times – Asia Pacific* in 2007 narrated his own experience:

'It's only 9 am here at Prem Dan, a long-term convalescent facility run by Mother Teresa's Missionaries of Charity, but already my fellow volunteers and I are soaked with sweat as we bend over tanks of water, hand-washing laundry for close to one hundred patients. It is hard work in the early June heat. Six volunteers are sloshing clothes around in soapy water; the rest, myself included, rinse and wring out the garments before they are taken to dry in the harsh pre-monsoon sunshine. As the old man, at 44, I initially fear that I won't be able to keep up with the 20-something guys around me, but I soon get the rhythm. There is a strong spirit of teamwork here, and when a wet shirt goes zipping by my ear, knocking my baseball cap into the water, I turn to face the grinning culprit and laugh with everyone else.

At Mother House, I meet volunteers from all over the world, including French, Italian, Japanese, Korean, Spaniards, Germans, Americans, Canadians and Irish. While there is naturally some cliquishness along national and linguistic lines, the common challenges help to bring the strangers together. Many volunteers are seasoned travelers, while others were outside of their home countries for the first time (I am stunned to find a couple of midwestern Americans violating a cardinal rule of Indian travel, eating raw salad in a local restaurant. Sure enough, they both go out of commission for forty eight hours). Some of the volunteers are medical professionals or social workers; there are quite a few office workers and many students. The youngest volunteer I meet is seventeen years old, the oldest is probably well beyond retirement age.

A social worker from Nebraska, Liz Wear, volunteering in Kolkata for the second time, urges me to work at some of the other facilities, as well. "You're not getting the 'true' experience," she nags in a friendly way.

So a few days later, I spend the afternoon working at a place called Nirmal Hriday. I approach it with trepidation. Kalighat, as it is also known, for the hindu temple complex with which it is associated, is the hospice for the dying that was the first of the facilities Mother Teresa founded here. It houses perhaps 150 patients in closely spaced beds, with men and women in separate wards. Most are old and sick, but no one is in obvious pain.'

Mother Teresa's Home for the Dying (Source: Marian Catechist Apostolate)

In 1990, Mother Teresa was asked to resign as head of the congregation but was soon voted back in as Superior General. On March 13, 1997, six months before Mother Teresa's death, Sister Mary Nirmala Joshi was selected the new Superior General of the Missionaries of Charity. Not concerned about the prospect of following in the footsteps of Mother Teresa, she has said, "I have to walk in my own shoes. We will continue as we have been doing." Inspired by Mother Teresa's works of charity, Sister Nirmala converted to Christianity at the age of twenty four. She took as her religious name a Hindi word that suggests a purity of mind and spirit. She has a master's degree in political science from an Indian university and additional training as a lawyer. She headed missions in Panama, Europe and in Washington DC, before being chosen to succeed Mother Teresa.

Controversy

Main controversy faced by the congregation was centered on the quality of care offered in various homes. *The Lancet* and the *British Medical Journal* reported the reuse of hypodermic needles, poor living conditions, including the use of cold baths for all patients, and an approach to illness and suffering that disallowed the use of many elements of modern medical care, such as systematic diagnosis. Volunteers are often untrained in medical practices and do not follow a systemic approach to treat and care for the patients. It was also observed that curable and incurable patients were not housed separately and those who had chances of surviving were constantly at risk of dying from infections and lack of treatment.

Another sensitive issue has been the donations received and the spending of charity money. One of her critiques, Christopher Hitchens has insisted that the donation money was not used by Mother Teresa on alleviating poverty or improving the conditions of her existing services but the expenditure was incurred on opening new convents and increasing missionary work. Also, the lack of transparency in accepting donations and the sources have been questioned. The Missionaries of Charity accepted donations from the autocratic and corrupt Duvalier family in Haiti and 1.4 million dollars from Charles Keating, involved in the fraud and corruption scheme known as the Keating Five scandal. The Deputy District Attorney for Los Angeles, Paul Turley, wrote to Mother Teresa asking her to return the donated money to the people Keating had stolen from, one of whom was 'a poor carpenter' but Turley did not receive a reply.

Mother Teresa has often been criticized for her views on suffering, which according to her would bring people close to Jesus. David Scott wrote that Mother Teresa limited herself to keeping people alive rather than tackling poverty itself. She was also criticized for taking a strong stance against contraception and abortion, glorifying poverty and alleged baptisms of the dying.

Colette Livermore, a former Missionary of Charity left the order on the grounds that she found Mother Teresa's 'theology of suffering' to be flawed. In her book, *'Hope Endures: Leaving Mother Teresa, Losing faith, and Searching for Meaning'*, Livermore wrote that she could not reconcile with some of the practices of the organization. Even though Mother Teresa insisted on the importance of spreading the message of Christ through service oriented actions instead of theological lessons, Livermore has cited instances when help was refused to the needy if they approached the nuns beyond the prescribed schedule. Nuns were not particularly encouraged to undergo medical training to enable them to deal with the illnesses they encountered. She also accused the congregation of imposing 'unjust' punishments on the inmates like being transferred away from friends. Livermore says that the Missionaries of Charity 'infantilized' its nuns by prohibiting the reading of secular books and newspapers, and emphasizing obedience over independent thinking and problem-solving.

In December 1996, a former nun in 'Mother' Teresa's order wrote the following letter (source: FBIS, 2/1/97):

'I myself was in Mother Teresa's order, the Missionaries of Charity. I am now a Christian. I was saved on 3/3/96... You are quite right about the pagan influences on the order. When I was a postulant in Rome, we had Hindu-style meditation techniques from a book called 'Sadhana' by Father Antony De Mello. Mother Teresa behaves like a Hindu guru. She visits each convent at six monthly to yearly intervals. The sisters seem to live for these visits and sit worshipfully at her feet when she gives one of her talks. On the special occasion when she presented us with our personal rosaries (in the postulancy in Rome) she said, 'My words are scripture for you,' and of course she was right. All the letters which she writes on 'spiritual' matters are kept, printed and copied and bound into volumes. Each convent has a copy of these volumes of her words which are studied daily as Christians study the Bible. Cuttings of Mother Teresa's hair and pieces of her saris are kept in a cupboard in Rome, ready to be made into relics when she is canonized.'

'But my main worry was the corporal penances used by the sisters and kept in small hand-made drawstring bags, along with toothbrush, needle and thread, etc. These include a whip made of rope and bracelets and waist-chains made of something similar to gardening wire which pierces the flesh. These penance implements are made by the novices in Rome. This is dangerous to the health, but is kept secret' (signed, Pamela Hursch, England).

Critiques have been frequently writing about the money made by Mother Teresa's orphanage services. According to a reporter (who pretended to be a volunteer), 'the Missionaries of Charity keep disabled children tethered to their cots and are unprofessional in providing medical care to their patients'. Sister Nirmala responded saying that criticism is welcome but we are alone with the children and no one is helping us.

Asia News interviewed some of the Missionaries of Charity who explained why, on rare occasions, they have to rely on extreme means. Understaffing is one reason; preventing children from hurting themselves is another.

Journalist Donal Macintyre went undercover in Daya Dan or Gift of Compassion Home where seven nuns are in charge of fifty nine children with different kinds of physical and mental disabilities, aged six months to twelve years. All the activities were filmed by him including the children being fed, hands bound with strips of cloth, recalling how, at night, they were tied to their cots with similar strips. He also filmed the children left unattended in the toilet, at times for up to twenty minutes.

In his view, most of the troubles were on account of poor training imparted to the sisters in dealing with disabled children. According to the journalist, one shackles animals or prisoners but definitely not children, especially those with special needs. Above all, he stressed, '(t)here are strategies for looking after disabled children that minimise stressful situations, but, as a result of poor training and lack of resources, staff are resorting to shocking practices.'

In an interview to an Indian TV channel, Sister Christie MC said: "Physical restraint is used only when absolutely necessary and for the safety of the child and (...) only and for a limited period."

It is because of Mother Teresa's image as a semi-God among people of all faiths that the government officials tread very carefully when it comes to investigations related to negligence despite the attention and focus of the international media on alleged insensitive handling of children. Mr Haque, Secretary of the Kolkata Social Welfare Department, told *Asia News* that "whenever any allegations are brought to our notice, we immediately investigate the case with some senior officer for the Department." Kolkata's Deputy Commissioner of Police N. Ramesh Babu added: "We will investigate and then take action. But firstly, we have to be sure and verify the allegations."

Sister Mariangelee MC, of Asha Dan in Byculla (central Mumbai), noted that in Daya Dan there are seven nuns for fifty nine children. "It may be," she said, "that in order to prevent them from falling and hurting themselves, they are secured with pieces of fabric as a precautionary measure... and not the brutal and cruel way that the story is portraying." She warned against generalising. "Please do not make it appear as if all handicapped children in all our homes are tied. You have to assess each situation differently; each home has a different context and different concerns." Sister Mariangelee explained that in their home children are not bound because 'we have enough volunteers to help us.'

When Mumbai was ravaged by the floods she said: "Our home was flooded knee-deep. We had to physically carry our children, all of whom are handicapped to a safer place. No one from the administration even came to inquire about the conditions of these children. We went without electricity and even water was scarce, but the authorities were nowhere in sight. Some of the children are so severely mentally handicapped, but by God's strength we managed to protect them from the perils of nature."

Sister Nirmala Joshi, Superior General of the Missionaries of Charity, sent *Asia News* an official statement in response to the journalist's allegations. Here it is:

'Thank you for bringing to our notice what you consider lapses in the quality of care and hygiene in this home. We value constructive criticism and admit that there is always room for improvement.'

It is only those who work day in and day out with these fifty–nine very special children who really know both the demands to total self-forgetfulness as well as the joy at the littlest response and improvement in these children.

God in His providence is supplying sufficiently for the needs of the poor under our care through the generous gifts of many individuals who make sacrifices to share in our work of love. Dedication, love, care is something money cannot buy and this is the reason our dearest Mother, Mother Teresa, encouraged people to give not just out of the abundance but their hearts of love and their hands to serve.

Our home continues to be simple, providing immediate and effective service to the poorest of the poor as long as they have no one to help them.

Physical restraints are used only when absolutely necessary for the safety of the child and for educational purposes for limited periods of time.

We try to provide all that is necessary for the physical, mental, emotional and spiritual needs of those under our care, and are committed to continual efforts at improving the quality of care we give them.

May God bless you and your efforts to promote the dignity of human life, especially for those who are underprivileged.*

This is a first hand account of a member of the congregation:

'As a Missionary of Charity, I was assigned to record donations and write the thank you letters. The money arrived at a frantic rate. The mail carrier often delivered the letters in sacks. We wrote receipts for checks of US $50,000 and more on a regular basis. Sometimes a donor would call up and ask

---

* 'British Journalist Makes Accusations Against the Sisters of Mother Teresa', Nirmala Carvalho, Asia News, August 3, 2005, http://www.asianews.it/index) php?art=3846&l=en.

if we had received his check, expecting us to remember it readily because it was so large. How could we say that we could not recall it because we had received so many those were even larger?

When Mother spoke publicly, she never asked for money, but she did encourage people to make sacrifices for the poor, to 'give until it hurts.' Many people did – and they gave it to her. We received touching letters from people; sometimes apparently poor themselves, who were making sacrifices to send us a little money for the starving people in Africa, the flood victims in Bangladesh, or the poor children in India. Most of the money sat in our bank accounts.

The flood of donations was considered to be a sign of God's approval of Mother Teresa's congregation. We were told by our superiors that we received more gifts than other religious congregations because God was pleased with Mother, and because the Missionaries of Charity were the sisters who were faithful to the true spirit of religious life.

Most of the sisters had no idea how much money the congregation was amassing. After all, we were taught not to collect anything. One summer, the sisters living on the outskirts of Rome were given more crates of tomatoes than they could distribute. None of their neighbors wanted them because the crop had been so prolific that year. The sisters decided to can the tomatoes rather than let them spoil, but when Mother found out what they had done she was very displeased. Storing things showed lack of trust in Divine Providence.

The donations rolled in and were deposited in the bank, but they had no effect on our ascetic lives and very little effect on the lives of the poor we were trying to help. We lived a simple life, bare of all superfluities. We had three sets of clothes, which we mended until the material was too rotten to patch anymore. We washed our own clothes by hand. The never ending piles of sheets and towels from our night shelter for the homeless we washed by hand, too. Our bathing was accomplished with only one bucket of water. Dental and medical check ups were seen as an unnecessary luxury.

Mother was very concerned that we preserve our spirit of poverty. Spending money would destroy that poverty. She seemed obsessed with using only the simplest of means for our work. Was this in the best interests of the people we were trying to help, or were we in fact using them as a tool to advance our own 'sanctity?' In Haiti, to keep the spirit of poverty, the sisters reused needles until they became blunt. Seeing the pain caused by the blunt needles, some of the volunteers offered to procure more needles, but the sisters refused.

We begged for food and supplies from local merchants as though we had no resources. On one of the rare occasions when we ran out of donated bread, we went begging at the local store. When our request was turned down, our superior decreed that the soup kitchen could do without bread for the day.

It was not only merchants who were offered a chance to be generous. Airlines were requested to fly sisters and air cargo free of charge. Hospitals and doctors were expected to absorb the costs of medical treatment for the sisters or to draw on funds designated for the religious work. Workmen were encouraged to labor without payment or at reduced rates. We relied heavily on volunteers who worked long hours in our soup kitchens, shelters and day camps.

A hard working farmer devoted many of his waking hours to collecting and delivering food for our soup kitchens and shelters. 'If I didn't come, what would you eat?' he asked.

Our constitution forbade us to beg for more than we needed, but, when it came to begging, the millions of dollars accumulating in the bank were treated as if they did not exist.

For years I had to write thousands of letters to donors, telling them that their entire gift would be used to bring God's loving compassion to the poorest of the poor. I was able to keep my complaining conscience in check because we had been taught that the Holy Spirit was guiding Mother. To doubt her was a sign that we were lacking in trust and, even worse, guilty of the sin of pride. I shelved my objections and hoped that one day I would understand why Mother wanted to gather so much money, when she herself had taught us that even storing tomato sauce showed lack of trust in Divine Providence.*

Hindu critics of Mother Teresa locate her work within the wider context of christian missionary activities in India, primarily religious conversion which they oppose. Right wing or nationalistic Hindus have been taking extreme positions when it comes to the issue of conversion especially

---

* 'Mother Teresa's House of Illusions', Susan Shields, Council for Secular Humanism, http://www.secularhumanism.org/index.php?section=library&page =shields_18_1).

in the state of Orissa. One critic, Ram Sita Goel, writes, 'The mischief created by Christian missionaries has to be seen to be believed... Mother Teresa is part of this gang, presenting India as a... diseased and corrupt country... and collecting fabulous sums for the machinery machine.' Arun Shourie, writing on how hindus view christians at the request of the Indian Catholic Bishops' Conference, argued that the Catholic Church in India spoke with a forked tongue; on the one hand it claims to be committed to inter-religious dialogue while on the other it spends vast sums aimed at converting hindus. In his view, this is the main reason why Christians in India engage in social welfare and educational initiatives. These are not offered in a spirit of unconditional service but in order to gain converts, which he says even devalues the work of Mother Teresa. Missionary work, he says, is not that noble after all. Mother Teresa, being a Catholic herself, believed that people should be free to convert but saw this as the work of the Holy Spirit, not as a human response. Her order's services are offered in love for people, with no strings attached or expectation of any particular response. Rather, they express unconditional love of the poor, despite Shourie's claim that conversion is the real objective.

Chapter 5

Declining Health and Demise

'On the last day, Jesus will say to those on His right hand, 'Come enter the Kingdom. For I was hungry and you gave me food, I was thirsty and you gave me drink, I was sick and you visited me.' Then Jesus will turn to those on His left hand and say, 'Depart from me because I was hungry and you did not feed me, I was thirsty and you did not give me to drink, I was sick and you did not visit me.' These will ask Him, 'When did we see You hungry, or thirsty, or sick, and did not come to Your help?' And Jesus will answer then, 'Whatever you neglected to do unto one of the least of these, you neglected to do unto Me!'

Mother Teresa moved with passionate intensity through the twentieth century, inspiring millions with her devotion to the poor and the ability to see the face of God 'in its most distressing disguise.' Her hectic schedules and constant physical strain involved in the nature of her work started affecting her health adversely. While visiting Pope John Paul II, she suffered a heart attack in Rome in 1983 and had to be put on an artificial pacemaker after the second attack in 1989. In 1991, after a battle with pneumonia while in Mexico, she suffered further heart problems. She offered to resign as the head of the congregation on account of failing health but the nuns of the order voted for her to stay in a secret ballot and she continued her work.

The year 1996 proved to be trying with her health causing major concern. Besides a broken collar bone, she also underwent a heart surgery. The Archbishop of Calcutta, Henry Sebastian D'Souza, said he ordered a priest to perform an exorcism on Mother Teresa with her permission when she was first hospitalized with cardiac problems because he thought she may be under attack by the devil. With constantly declining health, the controversial decision of getting Mother Teresa treated in California had to be taken. She stepped down as head of the Missionaries of Charity in March 1997 and the end came on September 5, 1997 in Calcutta at the age of eighty seven.

At the time of her death, Missionaries of Charity had extended its operations across the globe including hospices and homes for people with HIV/AIDS, leprosy and tuberculosis, soup kitchens, children and family counseling programs, personal helpers, orphanages and schools. As an expression of gratitude for her services to the poor in India, a state funeral was granted to her by the Indian government, prior to which she 'lay in state' in Kolkata for a week.

The city of Calcutta where Mother Teresa was cherished as a living saint was slowly absorbing the news of her demise. The spokesperson of Missionary of Charity said that the Nobel Laureate died following a heart attack. She reportedly complained of chest pain and breathing problems on friday evening but the doctors were unable to save her. Burial took place at the Mother House, the headquarters of the order she founded here almost half-a-century ago, on September 10, 1997.

Mother Teresa's graveyard

Thousands of people gathered outside Mother House in the early morning drizzle on saturday before filing past the body, which had already been embalmed before being laid out in the chapel. Sunita Kumar, one of her close associates said: "Mother will not leave Calcutta. She will be buried in Mother House." The funeral was scheduled for September 10, 'the inspiration day of Mother Teresa's life.' It was on that day that she opened her first home for the sick in Calcutta.

Indian Prime Minister Inder Kumar Gujral led the official memorials. "Words fail me to express my sorrow at the demise of the apostle of peace and love," he said. "The world—and especially India—is poorer by her passing away. Her life was devoted to bringing love, peace and joy to people whom the world generally shuns."

The world's top political and religious leaders joined in paying the tributes. The Vatican said that Pope John Paul II was 'deeply saddened' and would hold a special mass in her memory. US President, Bill Clinton called her 'an incredible person.' A message from Britain's Queen Elizabeth read: 'At this time of mourning for us in the United Kingdom, it was with deep sadness that I learnt this evening of the death of Mother Teresa. Her untiring devotion to the poor and destitute of all religions has been touched by her selfless work.'

Mother Teresa left an imprint on the hearts and minds of the people of the world. Will the vacuum ever be filled? Congregation believed that 'Mother's work is God's work, and even if Mother goes, God will be here. We'll miss her presence in the world, but God's not going anywhere.' More important than the person is the inspiration that came from her life and work.

In Rome, Douglas McLaren, of Caritas International, a Catholic humanitarian organization, said that, "The great thing that Mother Teresa has done is to put the plight of the extreme poor on the political agenda. I think her life has given an evangelical mission to the world. The world doesn't give forth a Mother Teresa too often, but I think that the underlying work, maybe in a quieter way, will go on." For Eileen Egan, a writer and retired veteran with Catholic Relief Services now in her eighties, the idea of a world without Mother Teresa is an invitation—and a challenge—for others to develop a mystic's vision. "It's something that all followers of Jesus should share," Egan said. "I think every religious person has to have a vision and live on the mystical level. I wouldn't like to think (Mother Teresa) is the only one."

Egan's 1986 biography of Mother Teresa, '*Such a Vision of the Street*' is drawn from personal experiences in the early 1950s, when she followed Mother Teresa on her rounds through the streets of Calcutta.

"She took me from the Home for Abandoned Children to the Leper Home to the Home for the Dying," Egan recalled in an interview a year before Mother Teresa's death. "I was just there for a few days. I said to her: How do you do this every day, day after day the same tragedy, the same suffering?" She said, "To me, each one is Jesus in a distressing disguise. "Jesus as leper. Jesus eaten alive by worms. Jesus in a distressing disguise. That struck me with tremendous force."

Egan has made an effort to analyze the reasons behind her popularity and honors conferred on her. "This little woman still stands for the inviolability and sacredness of each human person. That's what draws people to her. They want some sign that people aren't throw-aways. "A lot of people are wondering what is the meaning of my life," Egan said. "They see a woman who has nothing but love and is expressing it in works of mercy. They may not repeat what she's doing, but they do something in their own lives—even a smile."

Though Mother Teresa was best known for her charitable work, few people are aware of her anti-war activities, Egan noted. She read aloud a letter Mother Teresa wrote in 1991 to President Bush and Iraq's Saddam Hussein, urging them to pull back from the brink of war.

In Egan's mind, Mother Teresa's plea in that letter stands as a legacy for all willing to apply a mystic's vision to the world's miseries: 'I come to you with tears in my eyes and God's love in my heart to plead to you for the poor, and those who will become poor if the war that we all dread and fear happens,' Mother Teresa wrote. 'You (have) the power and the strength to destroy God's presence and image, his men, his women, and his children. Please listen to the will of God. In the short term there may be winners and losers in this war that we all dread, but that never can and never will justify the suffering, pain and loss of life which your weapons will cause.... I beg you please to save them,' she wrote. 'They are God's children'.

Mother Teresa's funeral on September 28, 1997

Reporting on September 5, 1997, BBC said that tens and thousands of people lined the route of Mother Teresa's funeral procession in Calcutta. 'Mother Teresa, the Nobel Peace Prize winner who devoted her life to helping the sick and the poor, has died at the age of eighty seven. She died of a heart attack at the headquarters of the Missionaries of Charity in Calcutta shortly before 1700 BST.' Revered by many around the world as a living saint for her work with the dispossessed, she was also praised by the Vatican. A Vatican spokesperson told media that the Pope was 'deeply hurt' by the news of her death and believes that 'she is a woman who has left her mark on the history of this century.' The head of the Catholic Church in England and Wales, Cardinal Hume, said she was an 'enormously significant figure – everyone knows who Mother Teresa is.' Her biographer and friend Navin Chawla said she would be remembered by the world as someone who 'gave the word compassion a new dimension.' At the time of her death, the order that she had founded and its national and international branches were serving more than 7000 children and sick people all over the world.

India Today – the cover story after Mother Teresa's demise

> The other day I dreamed that I was at the gates of heaven. And St Peter said, 'Go back to earth, there are no slums up here
>
> – Mother Teresa.

The slums remain but the Saint of the Gutters has gone. She was not ready. Eighty seven years old and fifty years of washing the brows of the dying, cradling women eaten by maggots, loving legless children abandoned by their parents was not enough for her. But her heart—regulated by a pacemaker since 1989 and failing fast in the past few years after a series of heart attacks—had to give way some day.

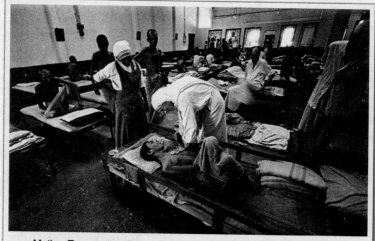

Mother Teresa attending to the patients at The Missionaries of Charity

On the morning of September 5, Mother Teresa complained of chest pain and was examined by her personal physician Dr Ashim Bardhan. But the pain persisted and, after a typically frugal dinner of bread and soup, an urgent summons was carried to Dr Alfred Woodward, an American doctor attached to the Missionaries of Charity, who rushed to her bedside. 'I cannot breathe,' is all she said. At about 9.30 pm, she died—like she lived—quietly. "We are drowned in despair," said Michael Gomes, at ninety-two the Mother's oldest friend, in whose modest house on 14 Creek Lane she had found the first shelter for her fledgling congregation in 1948. Cried Anukul Das, an old inmate of Nirmal Hriday, her Home for the Dying: "What will happen to us now?" Like him, the world was in shock.

Frail, tiny, soft spoken, always draped in the white sari with blue border, the uniform of her Missionaries of Charity, she was the world's most recognisable symbol of compassion. "I am here to convert hearts," she often said. She walked the South African townships, stood among earthquake victims in Armenia and comforted starving children in Colombia. But if she was Mother to the world's poor, it was India, especially Calcutta, that gave her work definition.

For Agnes Gonxha Bojaxhiu, born on August 26, 1910, the daughter of an Albanian builder, there was never any doubt where her life would go. At twelve, she decided to become a nun. At eighteen, she joined the congregation of Loreto nuns in Ireland. There, in that distant land, she would get the call to go to India. 'It's a mission country,' she explained later. And it was in Calcutta, where she arrived in 1929 to become a teacher at Loreto Entally school, that she had her first brush with poverty. Outside the high school walls were the Motijheel slums, and as she began to visit there, she said of those walls: "They seemed to me at that moment like a prison wall."

She broke through those walls eventually. On September 10, 1946, on a train journey to Darjeeling, she heard a 'call within a call.' As she explained then, 'The message was clear. I was to leave the convent and help the poor while living among them. It was an order.' Later, when the late journalist Desmond Doig, who wrote a book called 'Mother Teresa: Her People and Her Work,' asked her if she was ever in doubt, she replied, 'The conviction comes the moment you surrender yourself. Then there is no doubt.'

But she was tested. She would have to battle to be released from the Loreto Order and start on her own. Not everyone accepted her conviction. Then ,Archbishop

Ferdinand Periers was quoted as saying, 'I knew this woman as a novice. She could not light a candle in the chapel properly and you expect her to start a congregation?' But not for the first time was her steely will underestimated: her persistence paid off, and by 1950 she had set up the Missionaries of Charity.

Having taken the name Teresa from a sixteenth century nun called St Teresa, the patron of missionaries, she set for herself and her order a punishing life. The sisters own two sarees, a jhola, a pair of slippers; in the early days they kept only Rs 1.50 with them as they roamed the city searching for the dying. She lived first in Creek Lane and moved eventually to a building on Lower Circular Road, which came to be known worldwide as Mother House. Here too, life was spartan: despite the enormous donations that pour in, it has no washing machine, just one fan in the parlor (for visitors) and a phone simply because she was told it was truly a useful instrument. Her conviction was matched only by her organizational skills, her quizzical face masking a practical mind. In 1952, she opened her first home, Nirmal Hriday (literally 'Pure Heart'); today her Order works in 120 countries where it runs 169 educational establishments, 1,369 clinics and about 755 homes.

Critics said she was obsessed with poverty, that she lived off it, but made no move to remove it. Unshaken, Mother said, "You take care of their tomorrows, I take care of their todays." Feminist Germaine Greer once called her 'the glamour girl of poverty' and head of 'an order of clones'. The Mother said, "I will pray for her."

But not all the criticism could be swept away. She seemed outdated, her rigid anti-contraception stand perhaps naive, when she said, "I am fighting abortion with adoption." A 1994 British documentary Hell's Angel and a subsequent book accused Mother Teresa of denying pain killers to her dying patients due to her personal belief that physical suffering was good for spiritual well-being. The editor of the medical journal, The Lancet, said her staff made little effort to distinguish between the critically ill and those who could be cured.

Such criticism hurt. But no one could question her startling, almost abnormal, compassion. Not many cradle the diseased and dying. "The poor," she said, "do not want your bread, they want your love; the naked do not want your clothes, they want human dignity."

Everywhere she went, stories would emerge, legends would grow. How as a young sister she offered to work her own passage abroad as an air hostess; how she would tell air hostesses to pack up left-over food in a bag for children; how she asked the Nobel Prize organisers to cancel the traditional banquet and use the money to feed children. Perhaps because she was in a way the conscience of an apathetic world, because she made up for everyone else's inaction, no one dared shut the door in her face. The Prime Minister of Yemen, for instance, impressed by her work, lifted a 600 year old ban on Christian missionaries in the 1960s and invited her into his country. Though barely 5 feet at tiptoe, the rich, the famous, the powerful were dwarfed by her. Edward Kennedy wept in public; Indira Gandhi, out of power in 1978, found time in her hectic schedule to meet her; no one dared argue when she walked through the still-smouldering streets of West Beirut leading a group of orphaned children to their new home. The respect she earned was paid back through a heap of awards. The Nobel Peace Prize, the Leo Tolstoy International Award, the Bharat Ratna... the list is endless. To put it briefly, since the Nobel Prize in 1979, she received over fifty national and international awards. What did these awards mean to her? Consider this: when the Pope awarded her a limousine she auctioned it for charity.

So was Mother Teresa a saint? The world has already begun to talk of her canonisation. But according to the rules of the Catholic Church, decades may pass before she can be elevated to sainthood. It is a complicated process that requires at least two miracles after her death. That isn't a problem. Go to Nirmal Hriday and take a look at the faces of the once-despairing destitute. In their dignity lie all miracles.

Chapter 6
Mother Teresa's Thoughts

'With humor, compassion and lyrical clarity, Mother Teresa illuminates the sacred in the intimate everyday tasks of living.'

On Love and Compassion

'We will never know how much a simple smile will do... Let's not use bombs and guns to overcome the world... Let's love and let there be compassion... Peace begins with a smile... Let's radiate the peace of God and His light... It will extinguish all hatred from the hearts of the people... I want you to be concerned about your next door neighbor. Do you know your next door neighbour?...Be faithful in small things because it is in them that your strength lies.'

'Do not think that love, in order to be genuine, has to be extraordinary... What we need is to love without getting tired... Being unwanted, unloved, uncared for, forgotten by everybody, I think that is a much greater hunger, a much greater poverty than the person who has nothing to eat... Even the rich are hungry for love, for being cared for, for being wanted, for having someone to call their own... Every time you smile at someone, it is an action of love, a gift to that person, a beautiful thing... Good works are links that form a chain of love... I am a little pencil in the hand of writing God who is sending a love letter to the world... God loves the world through you and me... In loving one another through our works, we bring an increase of grace and a growth in divine love... I have found the paradox, that if you love until it hurts, there can be no more hurt, only more love... I try to give to the poor people for love what the rich could get for money... No, I wouldn't touch a leper for a thousand pounds; yet I willingly cure him for the love of God... If we want a love message to be heard, it has got to be sent out... To keep a lamp burning, we have to keep putting oil in it... If you judge people, you have no time to love them... In this life we cannot do great things. We can only do small things with great love. Intense love does not measure, it just gives.'

'It is not the magnitude of our actions but the amount of love that is put into them that matters... Jesus said love one another. He didn't say love the whole world... Love begins by taking care of the closest ones—the ones at home... Love is a fruit in season at all times, and within reach of every hand... Let us not be satisfied with just giving money... Love has a hem to her garment that reaches the very dust. It sweeps the stains from the streets and lanes. And because it can, it must... Money is not enough, money can be got, but they need your hearts to love them... So, spread your love everywhere you go...

The biggest disease today is not leprosy or tuberculosis, but rather the feeling of being unwanted... The success of love is in the loving – it is not in the result of loving...

Of course it is natural in love to want the best for the other person, but whether it turns out that way or not does not determine the value of what we have done... Let us more and more insist on raising funds of love, of kindness, of understanding, of peace... Money will come if we seek first the Kingdom of God—the rest will be given... There is always the danger that we may just do the work for the sake of the work... This is where the respect and the love and the devotion come in - that we do it to God, to Christ, and that's why we try to do it as beautifully as possible.'

On Care and Kindness

'In these times of development, the whole world runs and is in a hurry. But there are some who fall down on the way and have no strength to go ahead. These are the one's we must care about. Be kind in your actions... It is a kingly act to assist the fallen...Kind words can be short and easy to speak, but their echoes are truly endless... Do your best and trust that others do their best... And be faithful in small things because it is in them that your strength lies... If you can't feed a hundred people, then feed just one.'

'Let no one ever come to you without leaving better and happier. Be the living expression of God's kindness: indness in your face, kindness in your eyes, kindness in your smile... When Christ said: I was hungry and you fed me, he didn't mean only the hunger for bread and for food; he also meant the hunger to be loved. Jesus himself experienced this loneliness. He came amongst his own and his own received him not, and it hurt him then and it has kept on hurting him. The same hunger, the same loneliness, the same having no one to be accepted by and to be loved and wanted by... Each one of them is Jesus in disguise... Every human being in that case resembles Christ in his loneliness; and that is the hardest part, that's real hunger... Let us touch the dying, the poor, the lonely and the unwanted according to the graces we have received and let us not be ashamed or slow to do the humble work... Kindness has converted more people than zeal, science or eloquence. Pride destroys everything... If you are humble, nothing will touch you—neither praise nor disgrace, because you know what you are... If you are a saint, thank God. If you are a sinner, do not remain so.'

'Sweetest Lord, make me appreciative of the dignity of my high vocation, and its many responsibilities. Never permit me to disgrace it by giving way to coldness, unkindness, or impatience.'

On Poverty and Suffering

'There is much suffering in the world-very much. There is material suffering – that from hunger, homelessness, and all kinds of diseases but the greatest of them all is being lonely, feeling unloved, just having no one... Being unwanted is the worst disease that any human being can ever experience.'

'Our life of poverty is as necessary as the work itself. Only in heaven will we see how much we owe to the poor for helping us to love God better because of them.'

On Sincerity

'Accept each other as we are... Do not be surprised at or become preoccupied with each other's failure; rather see and find the good in each other for each one is created in the image of God... Jesus said 'I am the vine; you are the branches... The life giving sap that flows from the vine through each of the branches is the same... Do not wait for leaders; do it alone, person to person... God doesn't require us to succeed; he only requires that you try... I do not pray for success, I ask for faithfulness... Many people mistake our work for our vocation. Our vocation is the love of Jesus.'

'I know God will not give me anything I can't handle. I just wish that He didn't trust me so much... The miracle is not that we do this work, but that we are happy to do it... We ourselves feel that what we are doing is just a drop in the ocean. But the ocean would be less because of that missing drop.'

'There must be a reason why some people can afford to live well. They must have worked for it. I only feel angry when I see waste. When I see people throwing away things that we could use... When one comes in touch with money, one loses touch with God....One day there springs up the desire for money and all the things that money can provide.... the superfluous, luxury in eating, in dressing, trifles. Needs increase because one thing calls for another. The result is uncontrollable dissatisfaction.'

On Silence and Joy

'In the silence of the heart God speaks... If you face God in prayer and silence, God will speak to you... Words which do not give the light of Christ increase the darkness... It is only when you realize your nothingness, your emptiness, that God can fill you with Himself.'

'We cannot put ourselves directly in the presence of God if we do not practice internal and external silence. In silence we will find a new outlook, new energy and true unity.

Listen in silence…We are called to withdraw at certain intervals into deeper silence and aloneness with God. God cannot be found in noise or agitation. We need to find God, and he cannot be found in noise and restlessness. God is the friend of silence. See how nature – trees, flowers, grass-grows in silence; see the stars, the moon and the sun, how they move in silence... We need silence to be able to touch souls.'

'A joyful heart is the normal result of a heart burning with love. Joy is prayer, strength and love… Joy is a net of love by which you can catch souls… She gives most who gives with joy…To children and to the poor, to all those who suffer and are lonely, give them always a happy smile… The best way to show your gratitude is to accept everything with love.'

On Abortion and Adoption

'Any country that accepts abortion, is not teaching its people to love, but to use any violence to get what it wants.'

One of the most controversial of Mother Teresa's views was on the issues of abortion and adoption. She felt that the greatest destroyer of peace in the world is abortion because 'it is a war against the child, a direct killing of the innocent child, murder by the mother herself. And if we accept that a mother can kill even her own child, how can we tell other people not to kill one another? How do we persuade a woman not to have an abortion? As always, we must persuade her with love... The mother, who is thinking of abortion, should be helped to love, that is, to give until it hurts her plans, or her free time, to respect the life of her child. The father of that child, whoever he is, must also give until it hurts. By abortion, the mother does not learn to love, but kills even her own child to solve her problems. And, by abortion, that father is told that he does not have to take any responsibility at all for the child he has brought into the world. The father is likely to put other women into the same trouble... So abortion just leads to more abortion... Any country that accepts abortion is not teaching its people to love, but to use any violence to get what they want... Many people are very, very concerned with the children of India, with the children of Africa where quite a few die of hunger, and so on. Many people are also concerned about all the violence in this great country of the United States. These concerns are very good. But often these same people are not concerned with the millions who are being killed by the deliberate decision of their own mothers. And this is what is the greatest destroyer of peace today – abortion which brings people to such blindness. And for this I appeal in India and I appeal everywhere – 'Let us bring the child back.'

The child is God's gift to the family. Each child is created in the special image and likeness of God for greater things – to love and to be loved.'

'It is poverty to decide that a child must die so that you may live as you wish... As older people are called to God, only their children can take their places. But what does God say to us? He says: 'Even if a mother could forget her child,

I will not forget you. I have carved you in the palm of my hand.' We are carved in the palm of His hand; that unborn child has been carved in the hand of God from conception and is called by God to love and loved, not only now in this life, but forever. God can never forget us. The beautiful gift God has given our congregation is to fight abortion by adoption. We have already, from our house in Calcutta, over 3,000 children adoption. And I can't tell you what joy, what love, what peace those children have brought into those families. It has been a real gift of God for them and for us. I remember one of the little ones was very sick, so I sent for the father and the mother and I asked them: 'Please give me back the sick child. I will give you a healthy one.' And the father looked at me and said, 'Mother Teresa, take my life first than take the child.' So beautiful to see it – so much love, so much joy that little one has brought into that family. So pray for us that we continue this beautiful gift. And also I offer you – our Sisters are here – anybody who doesn't want the child, please give it to me. I want the child. I will tell you something beautiful. *We are fighting abortion by adoption - by care of the mother and adoption for her baby. We have saved thousands of lives.* We have sent word to the clinics, to the hospitals and police stations: 'Please don't destroy the child; we will take the child.' So we always have someone tell the mothers in trouble: 'Come, we will take care of you, we will get a home for your child.' And we have a tremendous demand from couples who cannot have a child – but I never give a child to a couple who have done something not to have a child. Jesus said, 'Anyone who receives a child in my name receives me.' By adopting a child, these couples receive Jesus but, by aborting a child, a couple refuses to receive Jesus. I know that couples have to plan their family and for that there is natural family planning. The way to plan the family is natural family planning, not contraception. In destroying the power of giving life, through contraception, a husband or wife is doing something to self. This turns the attention to self and so it destroys the gifts of love in him or her.'

'The so-called right to abortion has pitted mothers against their children and women against men. It has sown violence and discord at the heart of the most intimate human relationships. It has aggravated the derogation of the father's role in an increasingly fatherless society. It has portrayed the greatest of gifts—a child—as a competitor, an intrusion, and an inconvenience. It has nominally accorded mothers unfettered dominion over the independent lives of their physically dependent sons and daughters.' And, 'in granting this unconscionable power, it has exposed many women to unjust and selfish demands from their husbands or other sexual partners. Human rights are not a privilege conferred by government. They are every human being's entitlement by virtue of his humanity. The right to life does not depend, and must not be declared to be contingent, on the pleasure of anyone else, not even a parent or a sovereign.'*

---

* Mother Teresa – 'Notable and Quotable,' Wall Street Journal, 25 February,1994 p. A14)

Chapter 7

Mother Teresa—Stories

'The other day I dreamed that I was at the gates of heaven… And St. Peter said, go back to Earth, there are no slums up here.' (CNN quoting Mother Teresa)

These words, once spoken by Mother Teresa clearly describe the life and work of the late Roman Catholic nun and missionary known as 'The Saint of The Gutters.' Through the years, her fame as well as the magnitude of her deeds continued to grow.

'In the world of today, Mother Teresa has become a sign of God's love. Through her, God has reminded the world of His intense love—His thirst—for mankind and His desire to be loved in return.'

—Fr. Brian Kolodiejchuk, Missionaries of Charity

This is what Mother Teresa faced when she stepped out of the Loreto convent:

'It was a place where there was not even one tree for three thousand inhabitants, without a single flower, a bird, apart from vultures and crows—it was a place where children did not even know what a bush, a forest or a pond was, where the air was so laden with carbon dioxide and sulphur that pollution killed at least one member in every family; a place where men and beasts baked in a furnace for the eight months of summer until the monsoon transformed their alleyways and shacks into lakes of mud and excrement; a place where leprosy, tuberculosis, dysentery and all the malnutrition diseases, until recently, reduced the average life expectancy to one of the lowest in the world; a place where eighty five hundred cows and buffalo tied up to dung heaps provided milk infected with germs. Above all, however, it was a place where the most extreme economic poverty ran rife. Nine out of ten of its inhabitants did not have a single rupee per day with which to buy half a pound of rice…Considered a dangerous neighborhood with a terrible reputation, the haunt of Untouchables, pariahs, social rejects; it was a world apart, living apart from the world' (Langford).

Saints not just reflect God's light; they also echo His voice, calling humanity into the Divine embrace. By the time Mother Teresa won the Nobel Prize, Time magazine had already proclaimed her a 'living saint' on its front cover. Her stories depict various aspects of poverty—a starving family dividing its gift of rice with equally hungry neighbors, a homeless child sneaking out from one of her shelters to be 'home' with his mother on the streets and quite a few instances of rich people not just giving donations but working as volunteers in her order.

Mother Teresa's Missionaries of Charity, in the stage of its infancy, had to care for the bodies of the destitutes dying in the lanes and gutters of the city. A dirt floored room was rented in Moti Jhil where a few dying men and women were cleaned, fed and cared for until they recovered or passed on. Mother Teresa herself narrated some of her touching experiences.

'A woman lay dying on a Calcutta pavement. Her feet were half eaten away by rats and ants. She had been lying there for days and no one had taken any notice of her. Then a nun came along. She was a tiny woman, dressed in a white sari which hung loosely about her and covered her head. She walked quickly, for she was always in a hurry. Her name was Mother Teresa. When she saw the woman on the pavement she stopped. Full of pity, she picked her up and carried her into a nearby hospital for treatment. They told her there that the woman was too ill and poor to bother about. Besides, they had no room. Mother Teresa pleaded with them, but they said there was nothing they could do for her. However, she would not leave her patient, and set off for another hospital. But it was in vain. The woman died.'

This was not the only person or the only instance when Mother Teresa found people dying on the streets. There were plenty of them. 'There was an old man who was so thin he looked like a child. It was pouring with rain when Mother Teresa found him lying dead under a tree in a mess of sickness and blood. He was outside a hospital but no one had taken him in.'

There is so much suffering in the world and there is so little love. 'If we could only bring back into our lives the life that Jesus, Mary, and Joseph lived in Nazareth, if we could make our homes another Nazareth, I think that peace and joy would reign in the world.'

'One day I picked up a man from the gutter. His body was covered with worms. I brought him to our house, and what did this man say? He did not curse. He did not blame anyone. He just said, I have lived like an animal in the street, but I am going to die like an angel; loved and cared for. It took us three hours to clean him. Finally the man looked up at the sister and said, sister I am going home to God. And then he died. I have never seen such a radiant smile on a human face as the one I saw on that man's face.'

A story is told of a Hindu priest from the Temple of Goddess Kali in Mother Teresa's neighbourhood, who like many others had been discarded as a hopeless case by the hospitals and doctors. In this state of helplessness, he was left to fend for himself. When the sisters approached him and volunteered to help, he gave in with great reluctance. On his death bed, he reportedly said, "For many years I have worshipped the image of Kali. Today for the first time I have seen the face of the divine mother." (Briggs).

For those she was able to touch and heal, Mother Teresa converted Calcutta into a 'city of joy.' Many saw and many, from the beggar at her feet to the Nobel Committee understood. The draw, the mystery of her mission had started—a phenomenon had begun. In Calcutta's night, a light was shining.

Gradually, as the mission grew in foreign countries, young people from all over the world began to offer their help. These youth from developed nations were finding a new joy and sense of purpose within—they slowly discovered that 'while they were touching the poor of Calcutta, God Himself was touching the less accessible, less easily admitted poverty of their own souls.'

In the developed world, in Europe and the United States, the missionaries had to cope up with a new situation—a different kind of need. Mother Teresa explained, "I found the poverty of the west so much more difficult to remove. In the west, there is not only hunger for food, but a big hunger for love."

Mother Teresa never asked or expected the audiences to contribute to her work by sending a cheque. She always insisted upon and urged them to 'come and see' the work of her sisters and learn to spend time with the poor and needy. 'This was the challenge people faced, as they discovered that the tug of conscience and heart Mother Teresa awakened both frightened and fascinated them at once.'

Once, a successful businessman traveled to India to be a volunteer in one of Mother Teresa's shelters for a month. He was longing to meet her but could not do so until the day of his departure since Mother Teresa was traveling. When he did manage to get an audience with her, he burst into tears, feeling sad about his own lifestyle. Mother Teresa walked up to him and said, "Don't you know that God knows you are doing the best that you can."

'Some of my sisters work in Australia. On a reservation, among the Aborigines, there was an elderly man. I can assure you that you have never seen a situation as difficult as that poor old man's. He was completely ignored by everyone. His home was disordered and dirty. I told him, "Please, let me clean your house, wash your clothes, and make your bed." He answered, "I'm okay like this. Let it be." I said again, "You will be still better if you allow me to do it."

He finally agreed. So I was able to clean his house and wash his clothes. I discovered a beautiful lamp, covered with dust. Only God knows how many years had passed since he last lit it. I said to him, "Don't you light your lamp? Don't you ever use it?" He answered, "No. No one comes to see me. I have no need to light it. Who would I light it for?" I asked, "Would you light it every night if the sisters came?" He replied, "Of course." From that day on the sisters committed themselves to visiting him every evening. We cleaned the lamp, and the sisters would light it every evening.'

'Two years passed. I had completely forgotten that man. He sent this message: 'Tell my friend that the light she lit in my life continues to shine still. 'I thought it was a very small thing. We often neglect small things.'

'One evening we went out and rescued four people off the streets. One of them was in a desperate condition. I told the sisters, "You take care of the others. I will care for this one who is worse off." I did everything for her that my love could do. I put her into bed, and I saw a beautiful smile light up her face. She squeezed my hand and only managed to say two words, "Thank you." And then she closed her eyes. I couldn't help but ask myself there beside her body, "What would I have said if I had been in her place?" My answer was very simple. I would have said that I was hungry, that I was dying, that I was cold. Or I would have said that this or that part of my body hurt or something like that. But she gave me much more. She gave me much more. She gave me her grateful love. And she died with a smile on her face.'

'One day I visited a house where our sisters shelter the aged. This is one of the nicest houses in England, filled with beautiful and precious things, yet there was not one smile on the faces of these people. All of them were looking toward the door. I asked the sister in charge, 'Why are they like that? Why can't you see a smile on their faces?' (I am accustomed to seeing smiles on people's faces. I think a smile generates a smile, just as love generates love.) The sister answered, 'The same thing happens every day. They are always waiting for someone to come and visit them. Loneliness eats them up, and day after day they do not stop looking. Nobody comes.'

To be abandoned is an awful poverty. There are poor people everywhere, but the deepest poverty is not being loved. The needs could be material or spiritual. Hunger could be for bread of friendship. They may need clothing, or they may need the sense of wealth that God's love for them represents. They may need the shelter of a house made of bricks and cement or the shelter of having a place in our hearts.

Narrating her experience while visiting a family in Venezuela who had gifted them a lamb, she recalled that when she went to thank them, she discovered that they had a badly crippled child. Mother Teresa asked the mother her child's name and she received a very beautiful answer. "We call him 'teacher of love' because he keeps on teaching us how to love. Everything we do for him is our love for God in action."

'One day a novice in Rome came to me. She was crying. I asked her, 'What is the matter?' She had just come back from a family and said, 'Mother, I have never seen such suffering. They had nothing in the house. There was this terrible sickness, the terrible cancer, and I could do nothing. Please allow me to do a little bit of extra penance. I want to share in that suffering.' She was a young sister, scarcely three years in our congregation, but it was painful for her to see the suffering of the others.'

'Joy is prayer, Joy is strength. Joy is love. Joy is a net of love by which you can catch souls. God loves a cheerful giver. He gives most who gives with joy. The best way to show our gratitude to God and the people is to accept everything with joy. A joyful heart is the normal result of a heart burning with love. Never let anything so fill you with sorrow as to make you forget the joy of Christ risen. This I tell my sisters. This I tell you.'

'I never forget what happened to our sisters in Rome, where we work with the shut-ins. They go to the poor people's houses. (We clean the house and give them a bath, wash their clothes in the house and so on.)The sisters found someone left in a terrible condition. They cleaned his room and washed his clothes and gave him a good bath, but he never spoke. After two days he told the sisters, "You have brought God into my life, bring father also."

They went to the parish priest and brought the priest. That man, who never spoke, only that sentence he said, made his confession (he was Catholic). He made his confession after sixty years, and next morning he died. He had a beautiful death!'

The appearance of the diminutive nun, dressed in her conventional white sari with blue border stripes, always managed to grip the audiences everywhere. Wherever she went, crowds followed her, hoping to touch her clothing or hear her speak.

In Mother Teresa's own words, 'a business acquaintance once characterized my world-view as 'distinct' which she later downgraded to 'incredibly un-fun'. While others enjoyed cozy dinners for two at fifty dollars, I could not help but remember that this was more than most workers in Guatemala earned in an entire month. Yet another startling truth is that Americans spend $ 6 billion yearly on Christmas gifts for their pets- roughly equivalent to what the United Nations says it would cost each year for every child in the world to be in school.'

When Joseph Langford approached the Sisters and Brothers of the Missionaries of Charity stationed in Rome, he learnt that the key to understanding Mother Teresa lay in the two simple words she placed on the wall of her chapels around the world – Jesus' words from the cross: 'I thirst.' In Jesus crucified and thirsting, God was revealing his 'infinite longing' for His children, a longing just as keen as any man's thirst for water in the desert heat.

While no one disputed the importance of these words, their meaning in Mother Teresa's spiritual life was not clear. It was evident that something extraordinary had changed her life – something that had rekindled the inner fire. She had been graced with an overwhelming experience of God – an experience of such power and depth, of such intense 'light and love' that completely transformed her. A 'Call within a Call' – Sister Teresa had become Mother Teresa.

What had precipitated this transition had been an intimate encounter with the divine thirst – fuelling her work for the poor- for all of us. She had learnt that God not only accepts us with all our misery, but that he longs for us, 'thirsts' for us, with all the intensity of His divine heart, no matter who we are or what we have done.

The strong grace of 'Divine Light and Love' received on the train journey to Darjeeling on September 10, 1946, was the turning point in her life. The journey had begun—Missionaries of Charity had started—'in the depths of God's infinite longing to love and to be loved.'

Chpater 8
Mother Teresa's Prayers

> Our prayers should be for blessings in general, for God knows best what is good for us.
>
> —Socrates

Mother Teresa invariably insisted upon the need to pray and how everyone should find time for prayer and meditation. She sought the strength and inspiration required to complete the tasks that she believed to be the divine will, through prayers.

'DEAR JESUS, help me to spread Thy fragrance everywhere I go. Flood my soul with Thy spirit and love. Penetrate and possess my whole being so utterly that all my life may only be a radiance of Thine. Shine through me and be so in me that every soul I come in contact with may feel Thy presence in my soul. Let them look up and see no longer me but only Jesus. Stay with me and then I shall begin to shine as you shine, so to shine as to be a light to others.'

—From the video *Everyone, Everywhere*

God is one and He belongs to everyone. It was important for her that everyone is seen as equal and treated equally before God. The services provided by her congregation did not make a distinction between people of different faiths. Make us worthy, Lord, to serve those people throughout the world who live and die in poverty and hunger. Give them through our hands, this day, their daily bread, and by our understanding love, give them peace and joy, she prayed.

'There are so many religions and each one has its different ways of following God. I follow Christ:

Jesus is my God, Jesus is my Spouse
Jesus is my Life, Jesus is my only Love
Jesus is my All in All, Jesus is my Everything.

Mother Teresa - The Symbol of Love

I pray that you will understand the words of Jesus. 'Love one another as I have loved you.'

The Fruit of Prayer

The fruit of silence is prayer, The fruit of prayer is faith
The fruit of faith is love, The fruit of love is service
The fruit of service is peace

Love to Pray

Feel often during the day the need for prayer and pray.
Prayer opens the heart, till it is capable
of containing God Himself
ask and seek and your
heart will be big enough to receive Him
and keep Him as your own.

If We Pray

If we pray, we will believe;
If we believe, we will love; If we love, we will serve.

Prayer of Saint Francis

Lord, make me a channel of Your peace
that where there is hatred, I may bring love
where there is wrong, I may bring the
spirit of forgiveness
where there is discord, I may bring harmony
where there is error, I may bring truth
where there is doubt, I may bring faith
where there is despair, I may bring hope
where there are shadows, I may bring light
and where there is sadness, I may bring joy.

Lord, grant that I may comfort, rather than
to be comforted
that I may understand, rather that to be understood
that I may love, rather than to be loved.

For it is by forgetting self, that one finds
it is by forgiving, that one is forgiven
it is by dying that one awakens to eternal life.

For the world torn with strife and for individuals caught in their web of personal interests, Mother Teresa prayed for peace.

Prayer for Peace

Lead me from death to life, from lies to truth.
Lead me from despair to hope, from fear to trust.

Lead me from hatred to love, from war to peace.
Let peace fill our heart, our world our universe... peace,
peace, peace.
When we pray to God we must be seeking nothing –
nothing.

— Saint Francis of Assisi

Prayer to the Holy Spirit

Breathe in me, O Holy Spirit,
that my thoughts may all be holy
Act in me, O Holy Spirit, that my work too may be holy
Draw my heart, O Holy Spirit, that I love but what is holy
Strengthen me, O Holy Spirit, to defend all that is holy
Guide me then, O Holy Spirit, that I always may be holy.

Whatsoever You Do

When I was hungry, you gave me to eat;
when I was thirsty you gave me to drink.
Whatsoever you do to the least of
my brethren, you do it to Me.
Come and enter the house of My Father.

When I was a stranger, you opened your doors;
when I was naked, you gave me clothes.
When I was tired, you gave me peace;
When I was frightened, you calmed me down.
When I was small, you taught me to read;
when I was lonely, you gave me your love.

I was in prison, you visited me;
I was sick and you took care of me.
In a strange country, you gave me a home;
When I had no job, you found me one.
When I was wounded, you took care of it;
looking for friendship, you gave me your hand.

Whether I was black, or white or yellow;
mocked at or insulted, you carried my cross.
When I was old, you smiled at me;
when I couldn't find peace, you brought it to me.

You saw me: full of spit and blood;
dirty with sweat, still you said you knew me.
You were on my side in times of despise;
in the hour of joy, we were together.

Radiating Christ

Dear Jesus, help me to spread Your fragrance
everywhere I go.
Flood my soul with Your spirit and life.

Penetrate and possess my whole being so utterly that all
my life may only be a radiance of Yours.

Shine through me and be so in me that every soul I come
in contact with may feel Your presence in my soul.
Let them look up and see no longer me but only Jesus!

Stay with me and then I shall begin to shine as You shine,
so to shine as to be a light to others; the light,
O Jesus, will be all from You; none of it will be mine,
it will be You shining on others through me.

Let me thus praise You in the way You love best,
by shining on those around me.

Let me preach You without preaching, not by words,
but by my example, by the catching force,
the sympathetic influence of what I do,
the evident fullness of the love my heart bears to You.
Amen.
When you pray, rather let your heart be without words
than your words without heart.

— John Bunyan

Prayer to Our Lady

Mary, Mother of Jesus, give me your heart so beautiful, so pure, so immaculate, so full of love and humility that I may be able to receive Jesus in the Bread of Life, love Him as You loved Him and serve Him as You served Him in the distressing disguise of the poorest of the poor. Amen.

Remember...

Remember, o most gracious Virgin Mary, that never was it known that anyone who fled to your protection, implored your help or sought your intercession was left unaided. Inspired with this confidence we fly to You, o virgin of the virgins, our Mother. To you we come, before you we stand sinful and sorrowful. O Mother of the word incarnate, despise not our petitions, but in your clemency, hear and answer us. Amen.

Mother Teresa's United Nations Prayer

(Mother Teresa composed this prayer for the United Nations International Year of the Family)

Heavenly Father,
you have given us the model of life in the Holy Family of
Nazareth.
Help us, O Loving Father,
to make our family another Nazareth where love, peace and
joy reign.

May it be deeply contemplative, intensely eucharistic,
revived with joy.
Help us to stay together in joy and sorrow in family prayer.
Teach us to see Jesus in the members of our families,
especially in their distressing disguise.

May the eucharistic heart of Jesus make our hearts humble
like his
and help us to carry out our family duties in a holy way.
May we love one another as God loves each one of us,
more and more each day, and forgive each other's faults as
you forgive our sins.

Help us, O Loving Father, to take whatever you give and
give whatever you take with a big smile.

Immaculate Heart of Mary, cause of our joy, pray for us.
St. Joseph, pray for us.

Holy Guardian Angels, be always with us,
Guide and protect us.
Amen.

'Let me thus praise You (Jesus) in the way You love best: by shining on those around me. Let me preach You without preaching, not by words, but by my example, by the catching force, the sympathetic influence of what I do, the evident fullness of the love my heart bears to You.' Amen.

What we usually pray to God is not that His will be done, but that He approve ours.

— Helga Bergold Gross

When a man is at his wits' end it is not a cowardly thing to pray, it is the only way he can get in touch with Reality.

— Oswald Chambers

Mother Teresa's Prayer

I asked God to take away my pride, and God said, No.
He said it was not for Him to take away,
but for me to give up.

I asked God to cure my bedridden daughter,
and God said, No.
Her soul is in reliability, and a body will die however.

I asked God to grant me patience, and God said, No.
He said that patience is a by-product of tribulations. It
isn't granted, it's earned.

I asked God to give me happiness, and God said, No.
He said He gives me blessings; happiness is up to me.

I asked God to spare me pain, and God said, No.
He said that suffering draws me apart from worldly cares
and brings me closer to Him.

I asked God to make my spirit grow, and God said, No.
He said I must grow on my own.

I asked God to help me love others as much as
He loves me.
And God said, 'Ah, finally, you have the idea.'

I asked, and God gave me trials to make me stronger.
I asked for wisdom, and God gave me
problems to rack my brains.

I asked for courage, and God gave me dangers.
I asked for love, and God gave me the miserable who
needed my help.

I asked for goods, and God gave me opportunities.
I got nothing that I wanted, but I got everything I NEEDED!
God has heard my prayers.
Grow flowers of gratitude in the soil of prayer.

— Terri Guillemets

Saint Teresa is known as the Saint of the 'Little Ways,' meaning she believed in doing the little things in life well and with great love. She is also the patron Saint of flower growers and florists. She is represented by roses. St. Teresa's Prayer: 'May today there be peace within. May you trust God that you are exactly where you are meant to be. May you not forget the infinite possibilities that are born of faith. May you use those gifts that you have received, and pass on the love that has been given to you.... May you be content knowing you are a child of God. Let this presence settle into your bones, and allow your soul the freedom to sing, dance, praise and love. It is there for each and every one of us.'

'Dearest Lord, may I see you today and every day in the person of your sick, and, whilst nursing them, minister unto you.

Though you hide yourself behind the unattractive disguise of the irritable, the exacting, the unreasonable, may

I still recognize you, and say: 'Jesus, my patient, how sweet it is to serve you.'

Lord, give me this seeing faith, then my work will never be monotonous. I will ever find joy in humoring the fancies and gratifying the wishes of all poor sufferers.

O beloved sick, how doubly dear you are to me, when you personify Christ; and what a privilege is mine to be allowed to tend you.

Sweetest Lord, make me appreciative of the dignity of my high vocation, and its many responsibilities. Never permit me to disgrace it by giving way to coldness, unkindness, or impatience.

And O God, while you are Jesus my patient, deign also to be to me a patient Jesus, bearing with my faults, looking only to my intention, which is to love and serve you in the person of each one of your sick.'

Cardinal Angelo Sodano, the Vatican's secretary of state and the special envoy of Pope John Paul II, said Mother Teresa's life was a story of biblical faith that exemplified the teaching that it is more blessed to give than to receive. 'Mother Teresa of Calcutta understood fully the gospel of life', Sodano said. 'She understood it with every fiber of her indomitable spirit and every ounce of energy of her frail body'.'

Lord, increase my faith, bless my efforts and work,
now and for evermore, Amen.
'Behold, I stand at the door and knock... (Rev. 3, 20)

'It is true. I stand at the door of your heart, day and night. Even when you are not listening, even when you doubt it could be Me, I am there. I await even the smallest sign of your response, even the least whispered invitation that will allow Me to enter.

And I want you to know that whenever you invite Me, I do come—always, without fail. Silent and unseen I come, but with infinite power and love, and bringing the many gifts of My Spirit. I come with My mercy, with My desire to forgive and heal you, and with a love for you beyond your comprehension—a love every bit as great as the love I have received from the Father ('As much as the Father has loved me, I have loved you...') (Jn. 15:10) I come – longing to console you and give you strength, to lift you up and bind all

A Portrait of Jesus and Mother Teresa

your wounds. I bring you My light, to dispel your darkness and all your doubts. I come with My power, that I might carry you and all your burdens; with My grace, to touch your heart and transform your life; and My peace I give to still your soul.

I know you through and through. I know everything about you. The very hairs of your head I have numbered. Nothing in your life is unimportant to Me. I have followed you through the years, and I have always loved you – even in your wanderings. I know every one of your problems. I know your needs and your worries. And yes, I know all your sins. But I tell you again that I love you – not for what you have or haven't done—I love you for you, for the beauty and dignity My Father gave you by creating you in His own image. It is a dignity you have often forgotten, a beauty you have tarnished by sin. But I love you as you are, and I have shed My Blood to win you back. If you only ask Me with faith, My grace will touch all that needs changing in your life, and I will give you the strength to free yourself from sin and all its destructive power.

I know what is in your heart—I know your loneliness and all your hurts—the rejections, the judgments, the humiliations, I carried it all before you. And I carried it all for you, so you might share My strength and victory. I know especially your need for love—how you are thirsting to be loved and cherished. But how often have you thirsted in vain, by seeking that love selfishly, striving to fill the emptiness inside you with passing pleasures – with the even greater emptiness of sin. Do you thirst for love? 'Come to Me all you who thirst...' (Jn. 7: 37). I will satisfy you and fill you. Do you thirst to be cherished? I cherish you more than you can imagine – to the point of dying on a cross for you.

I Thirst for You. Yes, that is the only way to even begin to describe My love for you. I THIRST FOR YOU. I thirst to love you and to be loved by you – that is how precious you are to Me. I THIRST FOR YOU. Come to Me, and I will fill your heart and heal your wounds. I will make you a new creation, and give you peace, even in all your trials I THIRST FOR YOU. You must never doubt My mercy, My acceptance of you, My desire to forgive, My longing to bless you and live My life in you. I THIRST FOR YOU. If you feel unimportant in the eyes of the world, that matters not at all. For Me, there is no one any more important in the entire world than you. I THIRST FOR YOU. Open to Me, come to Me, thirst for Me, give me your life – and I will prove to you how important you are to My Heart.

Don't you realize that My Father already has a perfect plan to transform your life, beginning from this moment? Trust in Me. Ask Me every day to enter and take charge of your life. – and I will. I promise you before My Father in heaven that I will work miracles in your life. Why would I do this? Because I THIRST FOR YOU. All I ask of you is that you entrust yourself to Me completely. I will do all the rest.

Even now I behold the place My Father has prepared for you in My Kingdom. Remember that you are a pilgrim in this life, on a journey home. Sin can never satisfy you, or bring the peace you seek. All that you have sought outside of Me has only left you more empty, so do not cling to the things of this life. Above all, do not run from Me when you fall. Come to Me without delay. When you give Me your sins, you gave Me the joy of being your Savior. There is nothing I cannot forgive and heal; so come now, and unburden your soul.

No matter how far you may wander, no matter how often you forget Me, no matter how many crosses you may bear in this life; there is one thing I want you to always remember, one thing that will never change. I THIRST FOR YOU – just as you are. You don't need to change to believe in My love, for it will be your belief in My love that will change you. You forget Me, and yet I am seeking you every moment of the day – standing at the door of your heart and knocking. Do you find this hard to believe? Then look at the cross, look at My Heart that was pierced for you. Have you not understood My cross? Then listen again to the words I spoke there – for they tell you clearly why I endured all this for you: 'I THIRST...'(Jn 19: 28). Yes, I thirst for you – as the rest of the psalm – verse I was praying says of Me: 'I looked for love, and I found none...' (Ps. 69: 20). All your life I have been looking for your love – I have never stopped seeking to love you and be loved by you. You have tried many other things in your search for happiness; why not try opening your heart to Me, right now, more than you ever have before.

Whenever you do open the door of your heart, whenever you come close enough, you will hear Me say to you again and again, not in mere human words but in spirit. 'No matter what you have done, I love you for your own sake Come to Me with your misery and your sins, with your troubles and needs, and with all your longing to be loved. I stand at the door of your heart and knock. Open to Me, for I THIRST FOR YOU...'

'Jesus is God, therefore His love, His Thirst, is infinite. He the creator of the universe, asked for the love of His creatures. He thirst for our love... These words: 'I Thirst' – Do they echo in our souls?'

— Mother Teresa

Prayer for the Poor

Who is Jesus to me?
Jesus is the Word made Flesh.
Jesus is the Bread of Life.
Jesus is the Victim offered for our sins on the Cross.
Jesus is the Sacrifice at Holy Mass
for the sins of the world and mine.
Jesus is the Word - to be spoken.
Jesus is the Truth - to be told.
Jesus is the Way - to be walked.
Jesus is the Light - to be lit.
Jesus is the Life - to be loved.
Jesus is the Joy - to be shared.
Jesus is the Sacrifice - to be given.
Jesus is the Bread of Life - to be eaten.
Jesus is the Hungry - to be fed.
Jesus is the Thirsty - to be satiated.
Jesus is the Naked - to be clothed.
Jesus is the Homeless - to be taken in.
Jesus is the Sick - to be healed.
Jesus is the Lonely - to be loved.
Jesus is the Unwanted - to be wanted.
Jesus is the Leper - to wash his wounds.

Jesus is the Beggar - to give him a smile.
Jesus is the Drunkard - to listen to him.
Jesus is the Little One - to embrace him.
Jesus is the Dumb - to speak to him.
Jesus is the Crippled - to walk with him.
Jesus is the Drug Addict - to befriend him.
Jesus is the Prostitute - to remove from danger
and befriend her.
Jesus is the Prisoner - to be visited.
Jesus is the Old - to be served.

— Amen

Let us look now at the prayer which Mother Teresa wrote, and that every Missionary of Charity says before leaving for his or her apostolate. This prayer is also used as the Physician's Prayer in Shishu Bhavan, the children's home that Mother Teresa oversaw in Calcutta.

'Dear Lord, the Great Healer, I kneel before you,
Since every perfect gift must come from You.

I pray, give skill to my hands, clear vision to my mind,
kindness and meekness to my heart.

Give me singleness of purpose, strength to lift up a part
of the burden of my suffering fellow men, and a true
realization of the privilege that is mine.

Take from my heart all guile and worldliness,
That with the simple faith of a child, I may rely on You. '
(From A Simple Heart, by Mother Teresa. Published by
Ballantine Books, 1995)

Prayer for Canonization of Blessed Mother Teresa

Lord Jesus Christ, You made Blessed Teresa, an inspiring example of firm Faith and burning Charity, an extraordinary witness to the way of spiritual childhood, and a great and esteemed teacher of the value and dignity of every human life.

Grant that she may be venerated and imitated as one of the Church's canonized saints.

Hear the requests of all those who seek her intercession, especially the petition I now implore...

May we follow her example in heeding Your cry of thirst from the Cross and joyfully loving You in the distressing disguise of the poorest of the poor, especially those most unloved and unwanted.

We ask this in Your Name and through the intercession of Mary, Your Mother and the Mother of us all.

Chapter 9
Mother Teresa's Teachings

In addition to fulfilling her duties and the tasks that she took upon herself with love and devotion, Mother Teresa, besides being the greatest modern Christian missionary in the world, was also a teacher and preacher of love. The preaching of the *Good News* in a simple language touched the hearts of the masses.

'God does not demand that I be successful, God demands that I be faithful...Prayer does not demand that we interrupt our work, but that we continue working as if it were a prayer...Many people hope to change the world by changing institutions; rather we must change the world by changing ourselves...Every day, every hour, every single minute, God manifests Himself in some miracle...I wanted to be a missionary...to go out and give the life of Christ to the people... A missionary must be a missionary of love...Don't look for big things, look for small things and think what you can give to the society.'

'Put your love for God into living action, always remembering that it is not what you do, but what you are, and how much love you put into the doing, and have undivided love for God and each other...Charity must be given on a personal level, on a one to one basis...Do not allow yourselves to be disheartened by any failure as long as you have done your best.'

Her teachings were aimed at bringing about an attitudinal change towards people who are shunned by the society. 'Today, people with AIDS are the most unwanted and unloved brothers and sisters of Jesus; so let us give them our tender love and care and a beautiful smile...It's we who, with our exclusion and rejecting, push our brothers and sisters to find refuge in alcohol and become drunks. They drink to forget the deprivation of their lives.'

'With God, all things are possible...Start and end each day with prayer. Come to God as a child...My secret is quite simple: I pray...Prayer feeds the soul – as blood is to the body, prayer is to the soul – and it brings you closer to God. It also gives you a clean and pure heart...Pray for me that I do not loosen my grip on the hands of Jesus, even under the guise of ministering to the poor...It is faith in Jesus in the Eucharist that enables them (the Missionaries of Charity) to find Him also hidden in the hearts of the poor.'

'If we really understand the Eucharist, if we really center our lives on Jesus' body and blood, if we nourish our lives with the bread of the Eucharist, if will be easy for us to see Christ in that hungry one next door, the one lying in the gutter, that alcoholic man we shun, our husband or our wife, or our restless child. For in them, we will recognize the distressing disguises of the poor: Jesus in our midst.'

'Our intellect and other gifts have been given to be used for God's greater glory, but sometimes they become the very God for us. That is the saddest part. We are losing our balance when this happens. We must free ourselves to be filled by God. God cannot fill what is full.'

'I don't think there is anyone who needs God's help and grace as much as I do...The important thing is to follow God's way, the way he leads us to do something beautiful for him.'

To err is human, to forgive divine. To be able to forgive had a very important place in Mother Teresa's teachings. 'We need lots of love to forgive...But we need much more humility to ask for forgiveness...I want you to share the joy of loving...Forgiveness offers us a clean heart, and people will be hundred times better after it...If we really want to love, we must learn to forgive...If in your family, your young daughter or son has done something wrong, forgive them. Show them the forgiving heart of God.'

Her views on family and children were aimed at reviving family ties, love in relationships and strengthening bonds. Mother Teresa advocated the importance of using preventive measures to plan families and not resort to killing the unborn child. 'Abortion is murder in the womb. A child is a gift of God. If you do not want him, give him to me. I will look after him but do not murder him.'

'A child is the greatest of God's gifts to a family, because it is the fruit of the parents' love. It is so wonderful that God has created that child! To think also that God has created you and me – that poor person in the street, that hungry person, and that ragged person. He has created us all in his image, for love.'

'Every child has been created for greater things – to love and to be loved – in the image of God. That's why people must decide beforehand if they really want to have a child. Once a child is conceived, there is life, God's life. That child has a right to live and be cared for...Abortion destroys the center of God's love.'

'We are teaching Natural Family Planning to the beggars – you would be surprised what these good people can do. They came to our house to thank us. As poor and disfigured as they are, the lepers, disabled and sick, all said to me, 'we have come to thank you for allowing us to plan our family without committing sin.' Among these people were Christians and non-Christians...If people in the slums of Calcutta and other parts of the world can successfully space their families without committing sin or destroying the wonderful gift of life, you people here in America who have been blessed with so much kindness from God can do the same.'

'Today, the little unborn child has become the target, the destroyer of peace and love, because the mother herself kills her own child. We must not be afraid of the little, unborn child. We must encourage the joy of loving in the mother's heart...A nation that destroys the life of an unborn child, who has been created for living and loving, who has been created in the image of God, is in a tremendous poverty.'

'The family is a precious and beautiful gift of God, and let us make sure that we never destroy this beautiful gift but keep the family united through prayer, love and sacrifice.'

'Mothers are at the heart of the family. Children need their mothers. If the mother is there, the children will be there, too. For the family to be whole, the children and the mother also need the father to be present in the home.'

'Teach your children to love one another. Teach your children to have respect for each other. Teach your children to share. Teach your children, because nowadays, many schools do not teach these things.'

'When families are broken or disunited, many children grow up not knowing how to love and pray. A country where many families have been destroyed like this will have many problems. I have often seen, especially in the rich countries, how children turn to drugs or other things to escape feeling unloved and rejected.'

'No matter who says what, you should accept it with a smile and do your own work.'

– Mother Teresa

One of the criticisms leveled against her congregation was the baptism of the sick and the dying. Personally, her views and her service appeared to be secular. Mother Teresa believed that 'it is humiliating to ask people to change their religion as it is something that cannot be bought and sold. At the most what one can change is the hearts of the people for the better...No one can force (anyone for conversion)... no one can force anybody...I always say: If tomorrow God gives you the desire to know the Christian faith, then you are bound in conscience to look for it. But nobody can force you. Not even God himself can force you.'

Naveen Chawla, her long time friend and biographer recalled asking her once very bluntly, "Do you convert?" She replied, "Of course I convert. I convert you to be a better Hindu or a better Muslim or a better Protestant. Once you've found God, it's up to you to decide how to worship him" (*'Mother Teresa Touched Other Faiths,'* Associated Press, 9/7/97).

'We never try to convert those who receive (Aid from Missionaries of Charity) to Christianity but in our work we bear witness to the love of God's presence and if Catholics, Protestants, Buddhists or agnostics become for this better men – simply better – we will be satisfied. It matters to the individual what church he belongs to. If that individual thinks and believes that this is the only way to God for her or him, this is the way God comes into their life – his life. If he does not know any other way and if he has no doubt so that he does not need to search then this is his way to salvation.'

No one would deny Mother Teresa's marvelous and wonderful humanitarian work among the poor and neglected of the world. In an interview with a nun who worked with Mother Teresa, dying Hindus were instructed to pray to their own Hindu gods! (Reported in *Christian News*): "These people are waiting to die. What are you telling them to prepare them for death and eternity?" She replied candidly, "We tell them to pray to their Bhagwan, to their Gods."

Her perception of an educated person was not just someone with accumulated book knowledge—real education is when that knowledge finds practical application. 'Education becomes meaningful only when the message of knowledge is spread to the people in its real form...The education which teaches respect and dignity for human lives, regardless of the wide disparities existing among individuals, is the greatest education for the fellow human beings.'

'Give yourself fully to God. He will use you to accomplish great things on the condition that you believe much more in His love than your own weakness...I just take one day. Yesterday is gone. Tomorrow is not come. We have only today to love Jesus.'

'Happiness is the sign of a generous person. It is often the mantle of self-sacrifice. Joy is the surest way to announce Christianity to the world...You have to be holy in your position as you are, and I have to be holy in the position that God has put me. So it is nothing extraordinary to be holy. Holiness is not the luxury of the few. Holiness is the simple duty for you and for me. We have been created for that... Keep the joy of loving God in your heart and share this joy with all you meet, especially your family. Let us be holy; let us pray...If you are humble, nothing will touch you, praise nor disgrace, because you know what you are.'

For those not loved, Mother Teresa gave love; for those discarded, she gave care and shelter. It is for everybody to take up social responsibility. 'The laity (those who do not belong to the clergy) have their part to play. What we (priests and the religious community) can do, they cannot do. But they should be given a chance. A beautiful part of the Church is coming forward and giving them a chance. They too need the gift of bread of life...At the moment of death we will not be judged according to the number of good deeds we have done or by the diplomas we have received in our lifetime. We will be judged according to the love we have put into our work.'

There is a tendency to talk a lot about the poor – from development schemes of the governments around the world to non-governmental organizations; everyone seems to be discussing the needs of the underprivileged sections of the society. 'We talk very much about the poor, but very little to the poor. I have been told I spoil the poor by my work. Well at least one congregation (Missionaries of Charity) is spoiling the poor because everyone else is spoiling the rich.' It is a combined responsibility – each one has to be sensitized towards helping others. 'If I thought in terms of crowds, I would never begin my work. I believe in the personal touch of one to one.'

According to Mother Teresa, teachers and physicians have a very important role in this endeavor. 'Love comes out of a clean heart. The doctors must have a clean heart to love, clean eyes to see, and clean hands to touch the sick people. A doctor can never say, "I have no time" …To the sick people doctors are like God from whom they expect the love, compassion and tender touch. Patients not only expect medicine or the treatment from a doctor but love and sympathy as well.'

The ability and willingness to make sacrifices strengthened by faith is the secret of serving. 'A sacrifice to be real must cost, must hurt, must empty ourselves…Let us remember that love, in order to survive, must be nourished by sacrifices…You must give what will cost you something. This then is giving not just what you live without but what you can't live without or don't want to live without....Then your gift becomes a sacrifice.'

Mother Teresa said, 'I love all religions but I am in love with my own.' All religions have a belief that priests connect us with God by teaching us what is expected of us and interpreting the divine laws. 'Give us holy priests, and we Sisters and our families will be holy! Without priests, we have no Jesus. Without priests, we have no absolution. Without priests, we cannot receive Holy Communion....How pure the hearts of priests must be to be able to say, 'This is my body.' How pure their hands must be to grant absolution at any time! When we go to confession we go as sinners full of sin. And when we come back from confession, we come back as sinners without sin. How great for priests to have been chosen by Christ to guide our people!'

The sisters as well as the volunteers associated with Missionaries of Charity were required to follow stringent rules when it came to work and personal lives. 'We choose that. That is the difference between us and the poor. Because that will bring us closer to our poor people. How can we be truthful to them if we lead a different life?... If we have everything possible that money can buy, that the world can give, then what is our connection to the poor? What language will I speak to them? What language?... Now if the people tell me it is so hot, I can say, "you come and see my room..." Without our suffering, our work would just be social work, very good and helpful, but it would not be the work of Jesus Christ, not part of the Redemption...'

A comprehensive look at Mother Teresa's theology and beliefs is necessary since she has been labeled by many 'Christian' leaders as the greatest modern day example of Christianity. This is greatly facilitated by *Mother Teresa – A Simple Path,* which is considered to be 'a unique spiritual guide.' The Christian way has always been to love God and ones neighbor as oneself. Yet Mother Teresa has, perhaps with the influence of the east, worked out six steps to creating peace in ourselves and others that can be followed by anyone – even someone of no religious beliefs or of a religious background other than Christian – with no insult to beliefs or practices. This is why, 'when reading Mother

Teresa's words and those of her community, we may, if we choose, replace the references to Jesus with references to other godheads or symbols of divinity' (page xxviii).

Her six steps to creating peace are: silence, prayer, faith, love, service, and peace. For those who do not know if they believe much in anything, Mother Teresa suggested they try small acts of love towards others. She strongly believed in prayer for everyone. She found no problem praying with Hindus, Muslims and other faiths. Three pages of sample prayers are prefaced with, 'You could replace 'Jesus' by 'God' if you are not a Christian' (page 35).

In 184 pages, there was nothing stating that salvation was through Jesus alone. She wrote, 'I've always said we should help a Hindu become a better Hindu, a Muslim become a better Muslim, a Catholic become a better Catholic' (page 31). There is no attempt to let others know that Jesus is the only way. There is no hint that Mother Teresa or her sisters believed the narrow way Jesus preached (cf. Matt. 7:13-14). Rather than scripture, there was page after page of humanitarian testimonies. In fact, Mother Teresa had a different word of God – Sister Theresina put it this way, 'We pray the Rosary as we go out – it's our weapon, the word of God' (page 125).

Mother Teresa can be considered as both, a pantheist (the view that nature and God are identical) and a universalist (religious or theological beliefs with universal applicability). She, in fact went to the extent of calling atheistic communists children of God. Those who believe and sincerely follow their own religious faiths will be saved. She told Muslims and Jews that they worship the same God as Christians.

Mother Teresa was actively involved in 'Evangelization 2000'- a project aimed at spreading information about Christianity and 'spreading the Gospel.' It also emphasized and agreed upon the fact that all religions basically have similar tenets. The first issue of *New Evangelization 2000* featured Mother Teresa prominently with her photographs and one entire article entitled, *'Mother Teresa Promises Support.'* (reported in the 2/15/93, *Bold Truth Press)*. She was also scheduled to join the Dalai Lama and hundreds of other world religious leaders at the *Parliament of the World's Religions* in 1993 in Chicago and was scheduled to lead a closed session of key participants on future co-operative efforts among the world's religions, but was forced to cancel for health reasons.

Mother Teresa was also involved in various projects with New Agers – also referred to as New Age Movement, New Age Spirituality and Cosmic Humanism (a western social and spiritual movement seeking universal truth). In 1985, Mother Teresa attended a conference sponsored by the United Nations University of Peace whose featured agenda was a call to bring about the New World Order. Mother Teresa also participated in the 'Summit for Peace' in Assisi, Italy, in November 1986 which was represented by many different religions, including Hindu, Buddhist, Islamic, Shinto, Sikh and North American Indians – all of whom united in prayers for world peace (11/10/86, *Time* magazine, page 78-79).

Many people have called her a living saint but the formal process of canonization requires performing at least one miracle by the candidate. Beatification precedes canonization. A second miracle is needed for full sainthood, which in modern times is usually a medically certified cure that can be attributed to the candidate's intercession with God.

For becoming a Catholic saint, normally there is a five year wait before the process of 'sainthood' is pursued, but Pope John Paul II made an exception for Mother Teresa and the process began within a year of her demise. There are three steps to sainthood: veneration, beatification and canonization. Step two, which requires confirmation of a miracle, was dealt with by a twelve member inquiry tribunal that looked at alleged miracles caused by her, examining in particular, the disappearance of a malignant tumor from a village girl's stomach.

The Holy Bible does not specifically talk about a special class of saints who can hear and answer prayer. The word saint, in the scriptures refers to every 'born again' child of God.

In her diaries, Mother Teresa often mentioned that there were doubts plaguing her mind concerning religious and spiritual beliefs in the last fifty years of her life. An Italian newspaper once reported that 'The real Mother Teresa was one who for one year had visions and who for the next fifty had doubts – until her death.' In 1958 she wrote, 'My smile is a great cloak that hides a multitude of pains.' In another letter she said: 'The damned of hell suffer eternal punishment because they experiment with the loss of God. In my own soul, I feel the terrible pain of this loss. I feel that God does not want me, that God is not God and that he does not really exist.'

Undoubtedly, Mother Teresa is the twentieth centuries' greatest example of devotion to the poorest of the poor, and of Jesus Christ's commandment to serve the poor. She believed in focusing on one thing you need in life and say the following words with conviction in order to reach the goal:

Today there is peace within me.

I trust my highest power that I am exactly where I'm meant to be....

I see the infinite possibilities that are born of faith and belief and will not forget them.

I will use the gifts given to me, and pass on the Love that I have been given....

I will be proud knowing I am a child of God....

This presence is deep in my bones and expands to fill the Universe,

I give my soul the freedom to sing, dance and express the joy of knowing God.

It is there for each and every one of us, I put away any prejudice, malice, selfishness and let love express itself through me...

The Vatican's secretary of state and the special envoy of Pope John Paul II, Cardinal Angelo Sodano said that Mother Teresa's life was a story of biblical faith that highlighted the teaching that it is more blessed to give than to receive. She had fully understood the gospel of life with 'every fiber of her indomitable spirit and every ounce of energy of her frail body.'

Biblical belief is firmly tied into having loyalty to God, and this loyalty is proven by *obedience to God's commands and to His teachings*. Saving Faith is accepting Jesus Christ's lordship. There can be no salvation without accepting everything that Jesus taught with absolute belief and obedience. This is the essence of the Gospel of Jesus Christ: teaching everything Jesus taught, teaching nothing else.

Whether Mother Teresa lived and served according to the Gospel has been a matter of debate. It was not just the good done to humanity but the indoctrination – what was she teaching these poor people whom she was serving? Was Mother Teresa true to Jesus' teaching that He was the only way to heaven? Was Mother Teresa true to Jesus' teaching that He was the only way by which a person could come to God the Father?

Mother Teresa, while speaking about conversion to her biographer, Desmond Doig said, 'What we are all trying to do by our work, by serving the people, is to come closer to God. If in coming face to face with God we accept Him in our lives, then we are *converting*. What approach would I use? For me, naturally, it would be a Catholic one, for you it may be Hindu, for someone else, Buddhist, according to one's conscience. *What God is in your mind you must accept...*

There are many Hindu ladies who want our way of life, the life of poverty, prayer, sacrifice and service. They want the life of a missionary. But they wish to retain their faith, their own belief in God... We live that they may die, so that they may go home according to what is written in the book, be it written according to Hindu, or Muslim, or Buddhist, or Catholic, or Protestant, or any other belief... We give them whatever they ask according to their faith' (Desmond Doig, *'Mother Teresa: Her People and Her Work'*). The result was reaction from some groups which believed that she is not doing much to help the poor spiritually and damning them to hell by confirming them in their false religious beliefs.

What she preached and practiced was not Biblical Christianity. This is not Saving Faith. But if we carefully analyse the statement *'What God is in your mind you must accept,'* this very clearly is standard New Age teaching, which does not believe in absolute right or wrong and accepts that there are many correct paths to attain God. This doctrine also believes that each person is inherently good, is born with divine qualities and can be close to God by simply raising their consciousness level.

This is one way of examining and analyzing Mother Teresa's teachings and it is this outlook that gave her teachings worldwide acceptance. The other aspect is the teachings that were fundamental to her religious worshippers and sisters of the congregation, which they believed in with all sincerity. Most basic is the belief that as long as a sister obeys she is doing God's will. Another is the belief that the sisters have leverage over God by choosing to suffer. Their suffering makes God very happy. The third is the belief that any attachment to human beings, even the poor being served, supposedly interferes with love of God and must be vigilantly avoided or immediately uprooted.

These beliefs were not invented by Mother Teresa – they were in fact established in religious congregations before Vatican II—but she did everything in her power to enforce them. Sisters are so committed to accept these rules that what happens as a result seems to be inconsequential.

Chapter 10

Do it Anyway—The Paradox

Life is sometimes synonymous with challenges, which may appear to be insurmountable. Betrayals, disappointments, feeling of being let down at the workplace or by the loved ones – the list seems to be endless, often leaving us disillusioned as the good deeds go unnoticed and flaws are pointed out so easily. With the blink of an eye, all the good work and deeds done with good intention get washed out and are gone forever.

Sounds like cynicism – doesn't it? But even the optimists would agree that real life situations can be difficult and trying, and though they are unpredictable, we have to not only endure but also overcome the hurdles. The best way to deal with problems is to be at peace with oneself and not loose sight of one's goals. Our identity – who we are and how the world remembers us is usually determined by our ability to deal with adversities.

Mother Teresa, the saint, had successfully mastered the art of living with purpose, wisdom and gratitude. Deep down we usually know exactly what the right thing to do is in any situation. But if we simply do not want to do it, we will not have any trouble coming up with an endless list of lame excuses to justify not doing it. Do the right thing anyway. That's what saints are made from. The world is full of violence, injustice, starvation, disease and environmental destruction. Have faith anyway.

Following verses were written on the wall of Mother Teresa's home for children in Calcutta and the composition of these verses is widely attributed to her. Some people believe that same words were written on the wall of her room too.

People are often unreasonable,
irrational and self-centered.
Forgive them anyway.
If you are kind, people may accuse you of selfish,
ulterior motives.
Be kind anyway.
If you are successful, you will win some unfaithful friends
and some genuine enemies.
Succeed anyway.
If you are honest and sincere, people may deceive you.
Be honest and sincere anyway.
What you spend years creating,
others could destroy overnight
Create anyway.
If you find serenity and happiness, some may be jealous.
Be happy anyway.
The good you do today, will often be forgotten.
Do good anyway.
Give the best you have, and it will never be enough.
Give your best anyway.

In the final analysis, it is between you and God.
It was never between you and them anyway.

– This version is credited to Mother Teresa

And bears striking resemblance to a composition originally by Kent Keith but has been re-written with more spiritual emphasis. Following lines have been composed by Kent Keith. He called it *'The Paradoxical Commandments'* which were written in 1968 as part of a booklet for student leaders. It was originally called *'The Ten Paradoxical Commandments for Christians'*, and he wrote it when he was a ninteen year old sophomore at Harvard as part of a book for student leaders entitled *The Silent Revolution: Dynamic Leadership in the Student Council,* published by Harvard Student Agencies. *The Paradoxical Commandments* subsequently spread all over the world, and have been used by millions of people.

People are illogical, unreasonable and self-centered.
Love them anyway.
If you do good, people will accuse you of selfish ulterior
motives.
Do good anyway.
If you are successful, you win false friends and true
enemies
Succeed anyway.
The good you do today will be forgotten tomorrow.
Do good anyway.
Honesty and frankness make you vulnerable.
Be honest and frank anyway.

The biggest men and women with the biggest ideas can be shot down by the smallest men and women with the smallest minds.
Think big anyway.
People favor underdogs but follow only top dogs.
Fight for a few underdogs anyway.
What you spend years building may be destroyed overnight.
Build anyway.
People really need help but may attack you if you do help them.
Help people anyway.
Give the world the best you have and you'll get kicked in the teeth.
Give the world the best you have anyway.

The association of 'Do It Anyway' with Mother Teresa and Missionaries of Charity ensured the worldwide popularity of these verses since they expressed the spirit in which the members of the congregation lived their lives and served the people.

As Kent explains in his book, *Do It Anyway: The Handbook for Finding Personal Meaning and Deep Happiness in a Crazy World:*

'I found out about it in September 1997 at my Rotary Club meeting. We usually begin each meeting with a prayer or a thought for the day, and a fellow Rotarian of mine got up and noted that Mother Teresa had died, and said that, in her memory, he wanted to read a poem she had written that was titled 'Anyway.' I bowed my head in contemplation, and was astonished to recognize what he read – it was eight of the original ten *Paradoxical Commandments.*'

'I went up after the meeting and asked him where he got the poem. He said it was in a book about Mother Teresa, but he couldn't remember the title. So the next night I went to a bookstore and started looking through the shelf of books about the life and works of Mother Teresa. I found it, on the last page before the appendices in *Mother Teresa: A Simple Path*. *The Paradoxical Commandments* had been reformatted to look like a poem, and they had been retitled '*Anyway.*' There was no author listed, but at the bottom of the page, it said: 'From a sign on the wall of Shishu Bhavan, the children's home in Calcutta.'

'Mother Teresa, or one of her co-workers, thought that the *Paradoxical Commandments* were important enough to put up on the wall at their children's home, to look at, day after day, as they ministered to the children. That really hit me. I wanted to laugh, and cry, and shout – and I was getting chills up and down my spine. Perhaps it hit me hard because I had a lot of respect for Mother Teresa, and perhaps because I knew something about children's homes. Whatever the reason, it had a huge impact on me. That was when I decided to speak and write about the *Paradoxical Commandments* again, thirty years after I first wrote them.'

Kent Keith has been focused on helping people find personal meaning since he was a college student in the sixties. The *Paradoxical Commandments* are guidelines for finding personal meaning in the face of adversity.

Is it possible to relate to these commandments or do we want to escape? Sorrows, miseries, troubles, needy people – are we ready to take the challenge or it would be preferable to go for a vacation? These are the times when we need to look at 'Do it Anyway' and believe that we can make a difference.

There are many people in this world who take up great humanitarian acts and consistently strive towards sorting out the problems that the world is facing today. Mother Teresa did focus on major issues but her primary focus was on directing her efforts on small acts of kindness and helping people each day with love and care. She did not seek admiration but relentlessly and selflessly worked for the poor and the needy, setting an example to aspire for.

Mother Teresa developed a new way of looking at the downtrodden and underprivileged stratum. She believed in love, recognition of dignity of human life, which were achievable on an individual basis and the world responded. In a world where the rich ignore the poor, her message played a vital role. Mother Teresa kept talking about simple acts of kindness, understanding and respect and the need to spread love and support to those in need in whatever way we can. The small actions she spoke of proved that helping somebody is after all not such a daunting task.

'Life is not easy. But life is beautiful, even when it is difficult. The beauty comes from giving your best.' Another paradox that characterized her saintly life was her widespread use of images of light and darkness. Like Socrates, she realized that people were often so confused by the light that they turn away from its source. While Mother Teresa was one of the few people who could light up a Church with her sheer presence, her letters disclose her fear that her own light was being extinguished. In one letter Mother Teresa thanked Jesus for sending her the darkness because *I have come to love the darkness for I believe now that it is a very small part of Jesus' darkness and pain on earth.* In another entry, she wrote of her deep joy *that Jesus can't go anymore through the agony – but that He wants to go through it in me.* Some have interpreted that to mean that God rendered her empty inside in order to find Him in the needs of others. But no matter how long the darkness lasted, Mother Teresa accepted her emptiness as a part of her interior cross because she was confident Jesus would *fill what He had emptied.'*

'The judgments of the secular world are far too simple. They failed to understand that her internal suffering was an inevitable consequence of her fervent love for God. The world's failure is another illustration of the wide gap that exists between Mother Teresa's religious faith and a secular faith that longs for what theologian H. Richard Niebuhr described as *a God without wrath (who) brought men without sin into a kingdom without judgment through the ministrations of a Christ without a cross'* Mother Teresa of Calcutta – Official site)

For forty years, the *Paradoxical Commandments* have circled the globe, touching the hearts of millions of people. They became a law unto themselves for doing good despite people and circumstances. They have been put on walls and refrigerator doors, featured in speeches and articles, preached from pulpits, and shared extensively on the web. They have been used by business leaders, military commanders, government officials, religious leaders, university presidents, social workers, teachers, rock stars, parents, coaches and students. Mother Teresa thought the *Paradoxical Commandments* were important enough to put up on the wall of her children's home in Calcutta.

Dr Keith's third book on *Paradoxical Commandments* relates them to Christian faith and the Bible. Keith,being a person of faith himself, knows that people search for meaningful lives, and he uses his *Paradoxical Commandments* to help provide such meaning. Each chapter lists the commandment, then draws on a teaching of Jesus or other figures in the Christian Bible to help explain it. He uses the biblical stories of the prodigal son, David, Moses, Job and the 'good Samaritan,' among others, to illustrate the commandments. Keith's presentation is simple and straight forward, his links between each commandment and the Bible easy to understand.

Chapter 11
Crisis of Faith

Mother Teresa, in the acceptance lecture on the occasion of being conferred with Nobel Peace Prize in Oslo, delivered a message that everyone was expecting – 'It is not enough for us to say,' I love God, and do not love my neighbor,' she said, since in dying on the Cross, God had 'made himself the hungry one—the naked one—the homeless one.' Jesus' hunger, she said, is what 'you and I must find' and alleviate. She condemned abortion and bemoaned youthful drug addiction in the west. Finally, she suggested that the upcoming Christmas holiday should remind the world 'that radiating joy is real' because Christ is everywhere—'Christ in our hearts, Christ in the poor we meet, Christ in the smile we give and in the smile that we receive.' This was on December 11, 1979.

Jesus has a very special love for you. As for me, the silence and the emptiness is so great that I look and do not see, listen and do not hear, is what she said to the Reverand Michael van der Peet, in September 1979. Yet, less than three months earlier, in a letter to the Reverand Michael van der Peet, that is only now being made public, she wrote with fatigued familiarity of a different Christ, an absent one. "Jesus has a very special love for you," she assured Van der Peet. 'But as for me, the silence and the emptiness is so great, that I look and do not see, listen and do not hear, the tongue moves in prayer but does not speak... I want you to pray for me—that I let Him have a free hand.' 'The smile,' she writes, is 'a mask' or 'a cloak that covers everything.' Similarly, she wonders whether she is engaged in verbal deception. 'I spoke as if my very heart was in love with God—tender, personal love,' she remarks to an adviser. 'If you were there, you would have said, 'What hypocrisy.'

These two statements, eleven weeks apart, are excessively inharmonious. The first gave a glimpse of the Mother Teresa we all know; the second is both surprising and shocking. She seemed to be contradicting herself. An icon whose life and service always appeared to be inextricably linked to faith, God and prayer, was living a different spiritual reality in private. This came to light primarily through the book, *'Mother Teresa: Come Be My Light'* consisting of letters written over around sixty years. It is a posthumous autobiography that could cause the overall reconsideration of Mother Teresa's personality. Even though she wanted these letters to be destroyed, the church, overruling her wish, decided to preserve the correspondence. It so happened that for the last few decades of her life, Mother Teresa did not feel the presence of God—her public appearances did not give away this dilemma but inside, there was deep spiritual pain. She compared this experience to hell, full of darkness, loneliness and torture and she often doubted the existence of heaven and even of God. The absence was felt around the same time when she started the work amongst the poor and dying in Calcutta, as the book's compiler and editor, Reverand Brian Kolodiejchuk, writes, 'Neither in her heart nor in the Eucharist' did she feel the presence of Christ. The Vatican insisted that the revelations will not obstruct her path to sainthood.

Kolodiejchuk, the editor of the book, *'Come Be My Light'* recalled that no one knew how tormented she was and it is this revelation that has given a whole new dimension to the way people understand her. Kolodiejchuk was a senior Missionaries of Charity member and responsible for petitioning for her sainthood. Mr Kolodiejchuk gathered the letters as part of the process to make Mother Teresa a saint, and is responsible for arguing in her favor. He said the letters would show people another side of her life, and said that the fact that she was able to continue her work during such torment was a sign of her spiritual heroism. The book is not the work of some agnostic. In fact, the Church itself acknowledges certain dark periods in spiritual journeys of saints. The term 'dark night' of the soul was coined by the Spanish mystic, St. John of the Cross in the sixteenth century to describe a characteristic stage in spiritual growth of some saints or spiritual darkness within faith. Mother Teresa's namesake, St. Therese of Lisieux, called it a 'night of nothingness.' Reverand James Martin, an editor at the Jesuit magazine *America* and the author of *My Life With the Saints,* a book that dealt briefly with Mother Teresa's doubts commented that, 'I've never read a saint's life where the saint has such an intense spiritual darkness. Mother Teresa found ways and means to live with this, inner conflict, abandoning neither her work nor her beliefs.'

'Lord, my God, you have thrown me away as unwanted – unloved,' she wrote in one communiqué. 'I call, I cling, I want, and there is no one to answer, no, no one. Alone. Where is my faith? Even deep down right in there is nothing. I have no faith. I dare not utter the words and thoughts that crowd in my heart I am told God loves me, and yet the reality of the darkness and coldness and emptiness is so great that nothing touches my soul. Did I make a mistake in surrendering blindly to the Call of the Sacred Heart?' Saint Thomas the Apostle – the 'Doubting Thomas' – doubted that Jesus had risen from the dead until, according to scripture, he touches the wound of a resurrected Jesus. Christ himself wondered, 'God, why have you forsaken me' while on the cross, the Bible says. It is through these times, as even King David of the Old Testament Psalms shows us, that God tests our faith and shows what great things can be accomplished through perseverance through the pain, doubt and isolation.

Most analysts believe that it was this crisis of faith that prodded her to do great work. Inability to perceive or feel close to God did not imply absence of God. But this argument did not have many takers among the atheists. Christopher Hitchens, author of *The Missionary Position* says, "She was no more exempt from the realization that religion is a human fabrication than any other person, and that her attempted cure was more and more professions of faith could only have deepened the pit that she had dug for herself." Christopher Hitchens, views her writings as evidence that her public image was created primarily for publicity despite her personal beliefs and actions. Hitchens writes, 'So, which is the more striking: that the faithful should bravely confront the fact that one of their heroines all but lost her own faith, or that the Church should have gone on deploying, as an icon of favorable publicity, a confused old lady who it knew had for all practical purposes ceased to believe?'

Even though she experienced doubts and struggled over her religious beliefs, Mother Teresa continued to find strength and perseverance in prayer and the silent contemplation of Jesus Christ. 'If there be God—please forgive me. When I try to raise my thoughts to Heaven, there is such convicting emptiness that those very thoughts return like sharp knives and hurt my very soul... How painful is this unknown pain—I have no Faith. Repulsed, empty, no faith, no love, no zeal,... What do I labor for? If there be no God, there can be no soul. If there be no soul then, Jesus, You also are not true.' There is definitely a possibility of some misinterpretation. She felt the sentiment of losing closeness with God but her belief that God continued to work through her did not diminish.

After ten years of doubting, Mother Teresa felt a short period of renewed faith. At the time of the death of Pope Pius XII in the fall of 1958, praying for him at a requiem mass, she said she had been relieved of 'the long darkness: that strange suffering.' However, five weeks later, she described returning to her difficulties in believing.

Benedict XVI used her life story to clarify one of his main points: 'In the example of Blessed Teresa of Calcutta we have a clear illustration of the fact that time devoted to God in prayer not only does not detract from effective and loving service to our neighbor but is in fact the inexhaustible source of that service.' Mother Teresa specified that, 'it is only by mental prayer and spiritual reading that we can cultivate the gift of prayer.'

Mother Teresa's life shows influences of Franciscan spirituality even though there was no direct connection between Franciscan orders and Missionaries of Charity. Mother Teresa herself was a great admirer of St. Francis of Assisi and the peace prayer of St. Francis is recited by the Sisters of her congregation every morning during thanksgiving after Communion. St. Francis lived his life serving the poor, especially the lepers and emphasized poverty, chastity, obedience and submission to Christ. Time magazine was the first to highlight her dilemmas.

The letters created a stir but there were some of them who really shook the hornet's nest are what Doubleday called the 'dark letters.' Writing in 1953, Mother Teresa said, 'Please pray especially for me that I may not spoil His work and that Our Lord may show Himself – for there is such terrible darkness within me, as if everything was dead. It has been like this more or less from the time I started 'the work.'

The thoughts continued to be with her and again in 1956, she wrote, 'Such deep longing for God – and... repulsed – empty – no faith – no love – no zeal. (Saving) souls holds no attraction – heaven means nothing – pray for me please that I keep smiling at Him in spite of everything.' Quite often, she found it hard to pray. 'I utter words of community prayers – and try my utmost to get out of every word the sweetness it has to give – but my prayer of union is not there any longer – I no longer pray.' This phenomenon was seriously analyzed by Christian leaders across the world. The previously unpublished material was collected by Roman Catholic

Diana, Princess of Wales and Mother Teresa

authorities in Calcutta after her death. Mother Teresa, who was greatly admired by Diana, Princess of Wales, said in another letter: 'The damned of Hell suffer eternal punishment because they experiment with the loss of God.'

'It is not difficult to understand the source of Mother Teresa's spiritual suffering. The old adage warned the faithful to be careful of what they prayed for because they might get it. In 1951, Mother Teresa fervently prayed to join in Jesus' suffering on the Cross. She wrote that the *passion* was the only aspect of Jesus' life in which she wanted to fully partake. She wanted to drink from his *chalice of pain.* Jesus answered her prayer with some of the dark feelings of loneliness and abandonment that had accompanied His own suffering on His Cross. Years after her doubts had started, Mother Teresa asked Father Joseph Neuer, a noted theologian whom she met in the late 1950s for his counsel. He told her that there was no human remedy for her spiritual condition and she should not feel responsible for her feelings. He advised her that her feelings of abandonment mirrored Jesus' feelings in the Garden and on the Cross. Her craving for God was a sure sign of His hidden presence in her life. Mother Teresa had never realized that sharing His Passion would include the mental anguish He suffered on the Cross when He cried out to the Father, *My God, My God, why have You forsaken Me.* Father Neuer reminded her that all saints experience a Garden of Gethsemane. Like Jesus, they all beg to be spared this agony of the soul.

Mother Teresa's mental anguish is best explained through the idea of the *dark night of the soul.* In the dark recesses of her troubled soul, she was hounded by terrible thoughts that *God seemed absent, heaven empty, and bitterest of all, her own suffering seemed to count for nothing'* (Mother Teresa of Calcutta-Official site).

Mother Teresa's dark night of the soul was a matter of great interest to agnostics and atheists across the world. *'If I ever become a Saint – I will surely be one of 'darkness.' I will continually be absent from heaven – to (light) the light of those in darkness on earth.' Blessed Mother Teresa, 1962.* It was as if she was walking into a spiritual desert but far from damaging her reputation, the experience became the crucible of sanctity. Instead of leading her to darkness, it directed her towards the saving light. Revealing of the contradictions she faced will go a long way in helping ordinary mortals like us to deal with our own doubts and predicaments. Her critics have sometimes taken a position that Mother Teresa decided to give her life fully to the poor and the needy because she was convinced that there is no God to help them out. Living with irresoluble conflicts was not easy for Mother Teresa. According to her letters, Mother Teresa died with her doubts and it seems she had even stopped praying, as she once said. Revered by the poor, she is a saint, a kind spirit who lit our world while she was alive and will continue to do so till eternity.

'We are living in a materialistic society that is slowly poisoning itself with its spiritual denial, moral relativity and prurient pursuits. Mother Teresa can be a beacon of light to people who only believe in material progress. For a personal example of her inner spirit, the world need only look to convert Malcolm Muggeridge who made Mother Teresa an international sensation with his 1969 film, *Something*

Beautiful for God. Muggeridge was a restless agnostic when they met in Calcutta in 1968 for the film. She advised him that his longing for God was *forcing Himself to keep away from him because He loved him so much.* Despite her doubts, Mother Teresa's love for others never wavered. As Father Kolodiejchuk emphasized, Mother Teresa could have shut down her religious devotion in the face of her *interior darkness,* but she continued to rise every morning at 4:30 to praise Jesus. Sister Nirmala Joshi, director of the Missionaries of Charity, said the letters show, *not a failure of faith,* but only that having one's faith tested has always been an integral part of the Catholic faith. The world needs to understand this'(Mother Teresa of Calcutta Center).

Carole Zaleski in *'First Things'* wrote that Teresa converted 'her feeling of abandonment by God into an act of abandonment to God.' In many ways, her own sense of marginalization from God helped Mother Teresa to recognize loneliness in others. She realized that rejection and abandonment was not only the province of lepers, but present even in the inner life of those who appear to be successful and privileged.

Chapter 12
National and International Recognition

Mother Teresa's work has been recognized and acclaimed internationally and she has received many awards and distinctions. Her work inspired people to become a part of her Order and devote some part of their lives in service. During her lifetime and after her death, Mother Teresa was consistently listed by Gallup's List of Widely Admired People to be the single most widely admired person. In 1999, she was ranked as the 'most admired person of the twentieth century.' The former UN Secretary General Javier Pérez de Cuéllar, said: "She is the United Nations. She is peace in the world." Nawaz Sharif, the Prime Minister of Pakistan said that Mother Teresa was 'a rare and unique individual who lived long for higher purposes. Her life long devotion to the care of the poor, the sick and the disadvantaged was one of the highest examples of service to our humanity.'

Various prizes conferred upon Mother Teresa include the Pope John XXIII Peace Prize in January 1971. Pope Paul

VI presented her with a cheque worth £10,000 given by the Vatican as the first Pope John XXIII Peace Prize. She received the cheque and donated it for the construction of a leper colony in Madhya Pradesh on land donated by the Indian government.

She was conferred the Nehru Prize for her promotion of international peace and understanding in November, 1972. The Award consisted of a citation describing her as 'one of the most impressive manifestations of charity throughout the world.' It stated further that she had inspired a large number of devoted people all over the world to work with her in the service of the destitute, the uncared for and helpless people of the society.

She also received the Balzan Prize for humanity, peace and brotherhood among peoples (1979) and in 1973, Mother Teresa was awarded the Templeton Prize for Progress in Religion, which made her the first recipient of this prize. She was selected out of a total of two thousand nominations by a panel of judges representing the major religious traditions of the world, including Christianity, Judaism, Buddhism and Hinduism.

The Magsaysay award was given in 1962 for Peace and International Understanding along with a cheque of ₹ 50,000. She utilized this award money to buy the Children's Home in Agra.

In 1962, she also received India's second highest award the 'Padma Shri', from the President of India, Dr Rajendra Prasad. India's highest civilian award, the 'Bharat Ratna,' was awarded to her in 1980. She continued to receive major Indian rewards in successive decades including the Jawaharlal Nehru Award for International Understanding in 1972. She was the first and only person to be featured on an Indian postage stamp while still alive.

Other awards bestowed upon her included a Joseph P Kennedy Jr. Foundation award in Washington. The award was made up of a heavy glass vase engraved with a figure of St. Raphael and inscribed with the increasingly familiar words: 'To Mother Teresa, whose struggles have shaped something beautiful for God.'

In 1974, the Prime Minister of the Yemen Arab Republic presented her with a 'Sword of Honor'.

On October 23, 1975, she became a recipient of one of the first Albert Schweitzer International Prizes, awarded at the University of North Carolina, Washington.

In March, 1975, the United Nations Food and Agriculture Organization struck its Ceres Medals in recognition of Mother's 'exemplary love and concern for the hungry and the poorest of the poor.' The Medal showed Mother Teresa representing the Roman Goddess of Agriculture.

In June, 1975, Mother Teresa was awarded the 'Voice of America's International Women's Year Pin' for her work for the poor in India. She was appointed an honorary Companion of the Order of Australia in 1982, 'for service to the community of Australia and humanity at large.' Her acceptance of this and another honor granted by the Haitian government proved controversial.

At a special ceremony attended by over 700 people, on November 2, 1975, she was awarded an honorary Doctor of

Laws degree Antigonish, Nova Scotia. Reverend Malcolm Macdonell, the President of the University, paid rich tributes to her saying: "It is that very realization that makes all of us very keen on having you visit us. Not only do we need the blessing of your presence but the teachers and all of us, are as poor as the people to whom you are giving your life although our need and poverty are of a different kind. In every walk of life, inspiration is needed and we are no exception."

In the same year during 'International Women's Year', Shirley Williams, the then Secretary of State for Consumer Protection in the British government, and Maurice Strong, Executive Director of The United Nations Environment Program, Senator Edward Kennedy and Robert McNamara, head of the World Bank, added their support to the nomination of Mother Teresa for Nobel Peace Prize.

On March 3, 1976, Mrs Indira Gandhi, as chancellor of the Vishwa Bharti University, conferred on Mother Teresa, the University's highest honor, 'The Deshikottama' (Doctor of Literature) scarf in recognition of her significant contribution to the cause of human sufferings. Mrs Gandhi (then Prime Minister of India) commented on her, "She is tiny to look at, but there is nothing small about her." Other awards include the United States Presidential Medal of Freedom (1985) and the Congressional Gold Medal (1994), honorary citizenship of the United States, November 16, 1996 (one of only two people to have this honor during their lifetime), and honorary degrees from a number of universities.

In June, 1977, she was awarded an honorary Doctorate of Divinity from the University of Cambridge. In that year, Lady

Jackson personally resubmitted Mother Teresa's nomination for Nobel Prize. On October 17, 1979, Mother Teresa was awarded the Nobel Peace Prize, 'for work undertaken in the struggle to overcome poverty and distress, which also constitute a threat to peace.' On December 8, 1979, she landed at Oslo's international airport accompanied by Sister Agnes and Sister Gertrude to receive the prize. She refused the conventional ceremonial banquet given to laureates, and asked that the $6,000 cost of the banquet be diverted to the poor in Calcutta. The money permitted her to feed hundreds of needy for a year. She stated that earthly rewards were important only if they helped her help the world's needy. When Mother Teresa received the prize, she was asked, "What can we do to promote world peace?" Her answer was simple: "Go home and love your family."

The Norwegian Nobel committee, while deciding to confer the Nobel Peace Prize on Mother Teresa, recognized her work in bringing help to suffering humanity. The basic philosophy, when it came to Mother Teresa's life, was firmly rooted in Christian faith. The committee emphasized the spirit behind her activities and her personal attitude and human qualities. She had constantly highlighted the respect and dignity of individual existence and compassion without condescension. Mother had politely refused the heavy coats and fur-lined boots to protect against a temperature of ten degrees below zero, by the Nobel committee.

More than one thousand people welcomed her. She was given a reception the moment she landed at Oslo, by the Indian Ambassador in Norway. She was grateful for the gift as it would provide housing for the homeless and for leper families. Moreover, she was especially grateful for the 'gift of recognition of the poorest of the poor of the world.'

On December 10, 1979, in the presence of King Olaf V Crown Prince Harald, Crown Princess Sonja and many other dignitaries, Mother accepted the gold medal and the money, as she had accepted all other honors, 'unworthily' but 'gratefully in the name of poor, the hungry, the sick and the lonely.' On tuesday, December 11, all the newspapers in Oslo carried pictures of Mother Teresa on their front pages. From that moment she became 'Mother Teresa, the Nobel Prize Winner.'

This is what she had to say to the world in her lecture in Oslo while receiving the Nobel Prize:

'As we have gathered here together to thank God for the Nobel Peace Prize I think it will be beautiful that we pray the prayer of St. Francis of Assisi which always surprises me very much – we pray this prayer every day after Holy Communion, because it is very fitting for each one of us, and I always wonder that 4-500 years ago as St. Francis of Assisi composed this prayer that they had the same difficulties that we have today, as we compose this prayer that fits very nicely for us also. I think some of you already have got it - so we will pray together.'

'Let us thank God for the opportunity that we all have together today, for this gift of peace that reminds us that we have been created to live that peace, and Jesus became man to bring that good news to the poor. He being God became man in all things like us except sin, and he proclaimed very clearly that he had come to give the good news. The news was peace to all of good will and this is something that we all want – the peace of heart – and God loved the world so much that he gave his son – it was a giving – it is as much as if to say it hurt God to give, because he loved the world so much that he gave his son, and he gave him to Virgin Mary, and what did she do with him?'

'As soon as he came in her life – immediately she went in haste to give that good news, and as she came into the house of her cousin, the child – the unborn child – the child in the womb of Elizabeth, leapt with joy. He was that little unborn child, the first messenger of peace. He recognised the Prince of Peace, he recognized that Christ has come to bring the good news for you and for me. And as if that was not enough – it was not enough to become a man – he died on the cross to show that greater love, and he died for you and for me and for that leper and for that man dying of hunger and that naked person lying in the street not only of Calcutta, but of Africa, and New York, and London, and Oslo—and insisted that we love one another as he loves each one of us. And we read that in the Gospel very clearly—love as I have loved you—as I love you—as the Father has loved me, I love you—and the harder the Father loved him, he gave him to us, and how much we love one another, we, too, must give each other until it hurts. It is not enough for us to say: I love God, but I do not love my neighbor. St. John says you are a liar if you say you love God and you don't love your neighbor. How can you love God whom you do not see, if you do not love your neighbor whom you see, whom you touch, with whom you live. And so this is very important for us to realize that love, to be true, has to hurt. It hurt Jesus to love us, it hurt him. And to make sure we remember his great love he made himself the bread of life to satisfy our hunger for his love. Our hunger for God, because we have been created for that love. We have been created in his image. We have been created to love and be loved, and then he has become man to make it possible for us to love as he loved us. He makes himself the hungry one – the naked one – the homeless one – the sick one – the one in prison – the lonely one – the unwanted one – and he says: you did it to me. Hungry for our love and this is the hunger of our poor people. This is the hunger that you and I must find; it may be in our own home.'

'I never forget an opportunity I had in visiting a home where they had all these old parents of sons and daughters who had just put them in an institution and forgotten maybe. And I went there, and I saw in that home they had everything, beautiful things, but everybody was looking towards the door. And I did not see a single one with their smile on their face. And I turned to the Sister and I asked: how is that? How is it that the people have everything here, why are they all looking towards the door, why are they not smiling? I am so used to seeing the smile on our people, even the dying one smiles, and she said: This is nearly every day, they are expecting, they are hoping that a son or daughter will come to visit them. They are hurt because they are forgotten, and see – this is where love comes. That poverty comes right there in our own home, even neglect to love. Maybe in our own family we have somebody who is feeling lonely, who is feeling sick, who is feeling worried, and these are difficult days for everybody. Are we there, are we there to receive them, is the mother there to receive the child?'

'I was surprised in the west to see so many young boys and girls given into drugs, and I tried to find out why – why is it like that, and the answer was: because there is no one in the family to receive them. Father and mother are so busy they have no time. Young parents are in some institution and the child takes back to the street and gets involved in something. We are talking of peace. These are things that break peace, but I feel the greatest destroyer of peace today is abortion, because it is a direct war, a direct killing – direct murder by the mother herself. And we read in the scripture, for God says very clearly: Even if a mother could forget her child – I will not forget you – I have carved you in the palm of my hand. We are carved in the palm of His hand, so close to Him that unborn child has been carved in the hand of God. And that is what strikes me most, the beginning of that sentence, that even if a mother could forget is something impossible —but even if she could forget—I will not forget you. And today the greatest means—the greatest destroyer of peace is abortion. And we who are standing here – our parents wanted us. We would not be here if our parents would do that to us. Our children, we want them, we love them, but what of the millions. Many people are very, very concerned with the children in India, with the children in Africa where quite a number die, maybe of malnutrition, of hunger and so on, but millions are dying deliberately by the will of the mother. And this is what the greatest destroyer of peace is today. Because if a mother can kill her own child – what is left for me to kill you and you kill me – there is nothing between.

And this I appeal in India, I appeal everywhere: let us bring the child back, and this year being the child's year: what have we done for the child? At the beginning of the year I told, I spoke everywhere and I said: let us make this year that we make every single child born, and unborn, wanted. And today is the end of the year, have we really made the children wanted? I will give you something terrifying. We are fighting abortion by adoption, we have saved thousands of lives, we have sent words to all the clinics, to the hospitals, police stations – please don't destroy the child, we will take the child. So every hour of the day and night it is always somebody, we have quite a number of unwedded mothers – tell them come, we will take care of you, we will take the child from you, and we will get a home for the child. And we have a tremendous demand from families who have no children that is the blessing of God for us. And also, we are doing another thing which is very beautiful – we are teaching our beggars, our leprosy patients, our slum dwellers, our people of the street, natural family planning.'

'And in Calcutta alone in six years—it is all in Calcutta —we have had 61,273 babies less from the families who would have had, but because they practice this natural way of abstaining, of self-control, out of love for each other. We teach them the temperature meter which is very beautiful, very simple, and our poor people understand. And you know what they have told me? Our family is healthy, our family is united, and we can have a baby whenever we want. So clear—those people in the street, those beggars—and I think that if our people can do like that how much more you and all the others who can know the ways and means without destroying the life that God has created in us.'

'The poor people are very great people. They can teach us so many beautiful things. The other day one of them came to thank and said: you people who have vowed chastity you are the best people to teach us family planning. Because it is nothing more than self-control out of love for each other. And I think they said a beautiful sentence. And these are people who maybe have nothing to eat, maybe they have not a home where to live, but they are great people. The poor are very wonderful people. One evening we went out and we picked up four people from the street. And one of them was in a most terrible condition – and I told the Sisters: you take care of the other three, I take of this one that looked worse. So I did for her all that my love can do. I put her in bed, and there was such a beautiful smile on her face. She took hold of my hand, as she said one word only: Thank you—and she died.'

'I could not help but examine my conscience before her, and I asked what would I say if I was in her place. And my answer was very simple. I would have tried to draw a little attention to myself, I would have said I am hungry, that I am dying, I am cold, I am in pain, or something, but she gave me much more—she gave me her grateful love. And she died with a smile on her face. As that man whom we picked up from the drain, half eaten with worms, and we brought him to the home. I have lived like an animal in the street, but I am going to die like an angel, loved and cared for. And it was so wonderful to see the greatness of that man who could speak like that, who could die like that without blaming anybody, without cursing anybody, without comparing anything. Like an angel—this is the greatness of our people. And that is why we believe what Jesus had said: I was hungry—I was naked—I was homeless—I was unwanted, unloved, uncared for—and you did it to me.'

'I believe that we are not real social workers. We may be doing social work in the eyes of the people, but we are really contemplatives in the heart of the world. For we are touching the Body of Christ twenty four hours. We have twenty four hours in this presence, and so you and I. You too try to bring that presence of God in your family, for the family that prays together stays together. And I think that we in our family don't need bombs and guns, to destroy to bring peace—just get together, love one another, bring that peace, that joy, that strength of presence of each other in the home. And we will be able to overcome all the evil that is in the world.'

'There is so much suffering, so much hatred, so much misery, and we with our prayer, with our sacrifice are beginning at home. Love begins at home, and it is not how much we do, but how much love we put in the action that we do. It is to God Almighty – how much we do it does not matter, because He is infinite, but how much love we put in that action. How much we do to Him in the person that we are serving.'

'Some time ago in Calcutta we had great difficulty in getting sugar, and I don't know how the word got around to the children, and a little boy of four years old, Hindu boy, went home and told his parents: I will not eat sugar for three days, I will give my sugar to Mother Teresa for her children. After three days his father and mother brought him to our home. I had never met them before, and this little one could scarcely pronounce my name, but he knew exactly what he had come to do. He knew that he wanted to share his love.'

'And this is why I have received such a lot of love from you all. From the time that I have come here I have simply been surrounded with love, and with real, real understanding love. It could feel as if everyone in India, everyone in Africa is somebody very special to you.

And I felt quite at home I was telling Sister today. I feel in the Convent with the Sisters as if I am in Calcutta with my own Sisters. So completely at home here, right here.'

'And so here I am talking with you—I want you to find the poor here, right in your own home first. And begin love there. Be that good news to your own people. And find out about your next-door neighbor—do you know who they are? I had the most extraordinary experience with a Hindu family who had eight children. A gentleman came to our house and said: Mother Teresa, there is a family with eight children, they had not eaten for so long—do something. So I took some rice and I went there immediately. And I saw the children—their eyes shinning with hunger—I don't know if you have ever seen hunger. But I have seen it very often. And she took the rice, she divided the rice, and she went out. When she came back I asked her—where did you go, what did you do? And she gave me a very simple answer: they are hungry also. What struck me most was that she knew—and who are they, a Muslim family—and she knew. I didn't bring more rice that evening because I wanted them to enjoy the joy of sharing. But there were those children, radiating joy, sharing the joy with their mother because she had the love to give. And you see this is where love begins —at home. And I want you—and I am very grateful for what I have received. It has been a tremendous experience and I go back to India—I will be back by next week, the 15th I hope – and I will be able to bring your love.'

'And I know well that you have not given from your abundance, but you have given until it has hurt you. Today the little children they have —I was so surprised—there is so much joy for the children that are hungry. That the children like themselves will need love and care and tenderness, like they get so much from their parents. So let us thank God that we have had this opportunity to come to know each other, and this knowledge of each other has brought us very close. And we will be able to help not only the children of India and Africa, but will be able to help the children of the whole world, because as you know our Sisters are all over the world. And with this prize that I have received as a prize of peace, I am going to try to make the home for many people that have no home. Because I believe that love begins at home and if we can create a home for the poor – I think that more and more love will spread. And we will be able through this understanding love to bring peace, be the good news to the poor. The poor in our own family first, in our country and in the world.'

'To be able to do this, our Sisters, our lives have to be woven with prayer. They have to be woven with Christ to be able to understand, to be able to share. Because today there is so much suffering—and I feel that the passion of Christ is being relived all over again—are we there to share that passion, to share that suffering of people. Around the world, not only in the poor countries, but I found the poverty of the west so much more difficult to remove. When I pick up a person from the street, hungry, I give him a plate of rice, a piece of bread, I have satisfied. I have removed that hunger. But a person that is shut out, that feels unwanted, unloved, terrified, the person that has been thrown out from society – that poverty is so hurtable and so much, and I find that very difficult. Our Sisters are working amongst that kind of people in the west. So you must pray for us that we may be able to be that good news, but we cannot do that without you, you have to do that here in your country. You must come to know the poor, maybe our people here have material things, everything, but I think that if we all look into our own homes, how difficult we find it sometimes to smile at each other, and that the smile is the beginning of love.'

'And so let us always meet each other with a smile, for the smile is the beginning of love, and once we begin to love each other naturally we want to do something. So you pray for our Sisters and for me and for our Brothers, and for our co-workers that are around the world. That we may remain faithful to the gift of God, to love Him and serve Him in the poor together with you. What we have done, we would not have been able to do if you did not share with your prayers, with your gifts, this continual giving. But I don't want you to give me from your abundance; I want that you give me until it hurts.'

'The other day I received 15 dollars from a man who has been on his back for twenty years, and the only part that he can move is his right hand. And the only companion that he enjoys is smoking. And he said to me: I do not smoke for one week, and I send you this money. It must have been a terrible sacrifice for him, but see how beautiful, how he shared, and with that money I bought bread and I gave to those who are hungry with a joy on both sides, he was giving and the poor were receiving. This is something that you and I—it is a gift of God to us to be able to share our love with others. And let it be as it was for Jesus. Let us love one another as he loved us. Let us love Him with undivided love. And the joy of loving Him and each other—let us give now – that Christmas is coming so close. Let us keep that joy of loving Jesus in our hearts. And share that joy with all that we come in touch with. And that radiating joy is real, for we have no reason not to be happy because we have no Christ with us. Christ in our hearts, Christ in the poor that we meet, Christ in the smile that we give and the smile that we receive. Let us make that one point: that no child will be unwanted, and also that we meet each other always with a smile, especially when it is difficult to smile.'

'I never forget some time ago about fourteen professors who came from the United States from different universities. And they came to Calcutta to our house. Then we were talking about that they had been to the home for the dying. We have a home for the dying in Calcutta, where we have picked up more than 36,000 people only from the streets of Calcutta, and out of that big number more than 18,000 have died a beautiful death. They have just gone home to God; and they came to our house and we talked of love, of compassion, and then one of them asked me: say, Mother, please tell us something that we will remember, and I said to them: smile at each other, make time for each other in your family. Smile at each other. And then another one asked me: are you married, and I said: Yes, and I find it sometimes very difficult to smile at Jesus because he can be very demanding sometimes. This is really something true, and there is where love comes – when it is demanding, and yet we can give it to Him with joy. Just as I have said today, I have said that if I don't go to heaven for anything else I will be going to heaven for all the publicity because it has purified me and sacrificed me and made me really ready to go to heaven. I think that this is something that we must live life beautifully, we have Jesus with us and He loves us. If we could only remember that God loves me, and I have an opportunity to love others as he loves me, not in big things, but in small things with great love, then Norway becomes a nest of love. And how beautiful it will be that from here a centre for peace has been given. That from here the joy of life of the unborn child comes out. If you become a burning light in the world of peace, then really the Nobel Peace Prize is a gift of the Norwegian people. God bless you!'

It was as early as 1970s that Mother Teresa had become an international celebrity. Her fame can be in large part attributed to the 1969 documentary *Something Beautiful for God*, which was filmed by Malcolm Muggeridge and his 1971 book of the same title. Muggeridge was undergoing a spiritual journey of his own at the time. During the filming of the documentary, footage taken in poor lighting conditions, particularly the Home for the Dying was thought unlikely to be of usable quality by the crew. After returning from India, however, the footage was found to be extremely well lit. Muggeridge believed that this was a miracle of 'divine light' from Mother Teresa herself. Others in the crew thought it was due to a new type of ultra-sensitive Kodak film. Muggeridge later converted to Catholicism.

Statue of Mother Teresa in Skopje

Blessed Mother Teresa of Calcutta has been immortalized throughout the world in honor of her selflessness and unwavering devotion to the poor through museums and dedications of churches, roads and other structures besides awards and honors. In her native country, a memorial room (museum) was opened in the Feudal Tower in Skopje, a building where she used to play as a child. The museum has a significant selection of objects from Mother Theresa's life in Skopje and relics from her later life. In the Memorial room there is a model of her family home, made by the artist Vojo Georgievski. Next to the Memorial room, there is an area with the image of Mother Teresa, a memorial park and a fountain. Just at the edge of Skopje's city mall is the place where the house of Mother Theresa used to stand, the memorial plaque was dedicated in March of 1998, and it reads: 'On this place was the house where Gondza Bojadziu—Mother Theresa— was born on 26 August 1910.' Her message to the world is also inscribed: 'The world is not hungry for bread, but for love.'

In Albania, Mother Teresa's day (October 19) is a public holiday. The airport of Tirana, the capital of Albania, is the Tirana International Airport Nënë Tereza, named after Mother Teresa in 2002. The second largest square in Tirana, the largest being Scanderbeg Square and the biggest Civil Hospital was named after Mother Teresa.

The main street in Kosovo's capital Pristina is called Mother Teresa Street *(Rruga Nëna Terezë)*.

Musical tributes include an album compiled and released by Lion communications, featuring artists from across the globe paying tribute to Mother Teresa. It was called 'Mother, We'll Miss You'. Various parishes have Mother Teresa as their patroness like Mother Teresa parish, Dakota Dunes, SD, USA , Blessed Teresa of Calcutta parish, Woodinville,

Memorial plaque dedicated to Mother Teresa at a building in Václavské náměstí in Olomouc, Czech Republic

In December, 1992, in Kolkata, she received the United Nations cultural agency's peace education award to 'crown a life consecrated to the service of the poor, to the promotion of peace and to combating injustice.' She was presented a cheque of £ 50,000 by the UNESCO Director General. The money was used by her to set up a home for the handicapped near Kolkata. In the same year, the President of Albania, Mr Ramiz Alia, awarded the citizenship of Albania to

WA, USA , Blessed Teresa of Calcutta parish, Ferguson, MO, USA , Blessed Teresa of Calcutta parish, North Lake, WI, USA, Blessed Teresa of Calcutta parish, Limerick, PA, USA, Blessed Teresa of Calcutta Parish, Halifax, NS, Canada, etc. Many schools in United States and Canada have been named after her. A block of Lydig Avenue, between Holland and Wallace Avenues, located in the New York City borough of the Bronx was renamed Mother Teresa Way on August 30, 2009, honoring her and the borough's growing Albanian community.

Mother Teresa was honored by the Indian government with an official reception within the ramparts of Delhi's historic Red Fort. The other two dignitaries to receive this honor were Pandit Nehru and Indira Gandhi. The function was organized by a Hindu organization and was attended by all the dignitaries of the capital: the Prime Minister, cabinet and government officials, diplomats and businessmen.

In July, 1987, the film *'Mother Teresa'* made by two American sisters, Ann and Jeanette Petric, was awarded the Soviet Peace Committee Prize during the 15th International Film Festival held in Moscow. Yasser Arafat, President of the Palestine Liberation organization, presented her with a cheque of US $ 50,000 and invited Mother to the Holy Land and asked her to open 'Death with Dignity' homes in Bethlehem and Jerusalem. In August, 1992, in New York, she received the Knights of St. Columbus' Gaudium et Spes Award from Cardinal John O' Conner. In August, 1992, she was awarded with an honorary fellowship of the Royal College of Surgeons in Ireland.

Mother Teresa, who had once been forced to take a sad decision of not visiting her dying mother in her homeland as she wanted to serve the poor of the world. Mr Alia also created a 'Mother Teresa Prize' to be awarded to those who distinguished themselves in the field of humanitarian and charitable work. In January, 1993, she received the papal award 'Pro Ecclesia et Pontifice' and the 'U Thant Peace Award' for her 'Sleepless Service to humanity' in October 1994.

Chapter 13
The Miracles

It is often said that religion is for believers only. For those who believe, no proof is necessary. No evidence is enough for non-believers. Science is what the modern civilization is familiar with; the cause and the effect but many a times we encounter phenomenon which do not fall within this paradigm and seem to defy logic. These are miracles – all religions are fraught with such instances – the unexplainable. Rationalists have doubted the veracity of such claims and looked for scientific evidence where none existed. Mother Teresa was once asked to comment on such controversies. She said they are temporary and eventually pass.

On October 19, 2003, Pope John Paul II declared the beatification of Mother Teresa, a step closer in the process of pushing her towards sainthood. To achieve sainthood, there would have to be two miracles performed after the death of the candidate. What was this miracle and whether it was authentic or not—the whole process of Mother Teresa's beatification and canonization involved dealing with these questions.

The process of Mother Teresa's beatification which is the third step towards possible canonization started in 1997 after her death. This required the documentation of a miracle performed from the intercession of Mother Teresa. In 2002, the Vatican recognized as a miracle the healing of a tumor in the abdomen of an Indian woman, Monica Besra, following the application of a locket containing Mother Teresa's picture. Besra said that a beam of light emanated from the picture, curing the cancerous tumor. This claim has been opposed on the grounds that Besra's medical records containing sonograms, prescriptions and physicians' notes which are held back by the Missionaries of Charity are required to prove the veracity of the claim. The officials at the Balurghat Hospital where Besra was seeking medical treatment are claiming that they are being pressured by the Catholic order to declare the cure as a miracle.

In the process of verifying facts, the Vatican had undertaken the arduous task of going through published and unpublished information. Reverand Brian Kolodiejchuk, the chief advocate of the case said that the Vatican's Congregation for the Causes of Saints interviewed 113 people and gathered evidence to the tune of around 35000 pages, attesting the virtues of Mother Teresa. It was also important to consider criticisms leveled against her by the rationalists. Christopher Hitchens was the only witness called by the Vatican to give evidence against Mother Teresa's beatification and canonization process, as the Vatican had abolished the traditional 'devil's advocate'role, which fulfilled a similar purpose. Hitchens has argued that 'her intention was not to help people,' and he alleged that she lied to donors about the use of their contributions. "It was by talking to her that I discovered, and she assured me, that she wasn't working to alleviate poverty," says Hitchens. 'She was working to expand the number of Catholics. She said, "I'm not a social worker. I don't do it for this reason. I do it for Christ. I do it for the church." Hitchens' allegations were examined and no obstacles were found to Mother Teresa's beatification and the title of 'Blessed' was conferred upon her.

Monica Besra said that she was a living proof of the miracle performed by Mother Teresa from heaven. Besra was not alone – millions of people in the slums of Calcutta spoke for the sainthood of the Roman Catholic nun who was a living saint for them.

Besra, a tribal woman from the village of Nakor, 450 kms north of Calcutta, said in an interview that the miracle which saved her life began with a vision. What exactly was the ailment she suffered from is not clear – some reports say that she had a large cancerous tumor in her abdomen; other reports indicate that it was tuberculosis. She was put on four anti-tubercular drugs, said Dr Ranjan Mustafi, the chief gynecologist who treated Besra at Balurghat District Hospital. Mustafi said that Mother Teresa was full of virtues but did not perform any miracles. Besra was poor and not able to take care of herself. Her family took her to the Missionaries of Charity hospice in Patiram, a town on the outskirts of Balurghat. On September 5, 1998 on the occasion of Mother Teresa's first death anniversary, the sisters urged her to come for prayers in the chapel.

"When I went in for the prayers and looked at a photograph of Mother Teresa, I saw rays of light coming from her eyes and I felt very light and dizzy," said Besra, speaking to journalists. This was the same story she had narrated to Vatican investigators and skeptical doctors hundreds of times. "I started shaking and my heart was beating very fast. I felt scared as I didn't know what was happening to me."

She was helped to go to bed and at around 5 pm, a small medallion of Mother Mary was put on the large lump in her right abdomen and she was asked to pray. "At 1 am the next morning, I awoke with a start and suddenly felt so light," said Besra. "I was so excited, I woke up the woman in the bed next to me, Simira", and told her, "Look, it's gone!" Her whole family has converted to Catholicism after this incident. Kolodiejchuk said five doctors in Rome were asked their medical opinion about Besra. 'The unanimous opinion of the doctors here was that there was no medical explanation for it.' These claims greatly upset members of the Science and Rationalists' Association of India who are primarily engaged in exposing charlatans and gurus offering miracle cures. In fact, members of an Indian rationalist group went to the extent of demanding the arrest of the head of Mother Teresa's congregation arguing that the facts relating to the claim of a miracle that is being cited to secure sainthood for her have been fudged. Prabir Ghose, general secretary of the group said, "Look Coca Cola promotes their business and that's what Sister Nirmala is doing. Sister Nirmala is a good businessman, nothing more." For many years Prabir Ghose had been challenging Hindu Godmen and spoke of miracles as 'cheap hypnotic tricks better performed by magicians.' Such skepticism was of course quickly discarded by the order. Prabir Ghosh went to the extent of saying that the forum registered fraud cases with the police against Sister Nirmala. The group claimed that the woman reportedly cured of cancer by placing a photograph of the nun on the abdomen had subsequently received treatment in government hospitals. The doctors who treated her say that she continued to be in pain years after Mother Teresa's demise. But the miracle was approved by the Vatican officials. Mr Ghose described the claim as bogus and 'typical of the process of cult building in all religious orders.' He says Mother Teresa could be considered for sainthood for her services to the poor, adding that it was an insult to her legacy to bestow her sainthood on false claims of miracles. According to him, there was evidence of Besra being admitted to a hospital with chronic headaches and severe abdominal pain at least a year after Mother Teresa's death. Deeming this cure as a miracle would generate and strengthen superstitious beliefs. Further, Mr Ghose urged the West Bengal government to take legal action against the Missionaries of Charity, hoping that the state would promote rational and scientific thinking.

How would one test the claim of Monica Besra? Some believed that this miracle happened, while others do not. What are certain facts surrounding the event that can verify or falsify this miraculous claim? These are the questions that need to be examined. Seeking the truth in these matters can pose tremendous challenges. Monica Besra's own husband's testimony denying that any miracles happened; Monica Besra's doctors testifying of her being healed by them; West Bengal government investigation concluding that medication healed her. If all this is true, then we would be forced to agree and fall in line with the rationalists.

Monica Besra's husband, in his testimony contradicted his wife. "It is much ado about nothing," he told the *Time* magazine. "My wife was cured by the doctors and not by any miracle." Besra's husband Sekhu Murmu has consistently rejected claims that his wife was cured by a miracle. He told reporters that he believed his wife had been cured by medication and not by a miracle.

"She did feel less pain one night when she used the locket, but her pain had been coming and going. Then she went to the doctors, and they cured her." They say there is a simple, scientific explanation and that Besra's tumor was in fact a tubercular lump, the disappearance of which can be attributed to prescribed drugs.'

These statements made by Besra's husband clearly indicate that he does not believe anything supernatural happened and that he described his wife's healing as an act of being 'cured by the doctors and not any miracle.' Later, he modified his testimony, as indicated in the London Telegraph news article by David Orr in Calcutta, probably due to pressures and material considerations.

"I'm very proud of my wife," he says of Monica Besra, a Bengali tribal woman who is leaving for Rome to attend Mother Teresa's beatification by the Pope in two weeks' time. "A few years ago we had never been outside our district in West Bengal. Now she will be travelling to this far-off place and she will see many new things." "Our situation was terrible and we didn't know what to do. Now my children are being educated with the help of the nuns and I have been able to buy a small piece of land. Everything has changed for the better."

According to some media reports, the doctors who treated Besra and other authorities in West Bengal rejected the miracle theory and believed that the whole episode was an elaborate hoax. "This miracle claim is absolute nonsense and should be condemned by everyone," Dr Ranjan Kumar Mustafi, of Balurghat Hospital in West Bengal, said. "She had a medium-sized tumor in her lower abdomen caused by tuberculosis. The drugs she was given eventually reduced the cystic mass and it disappeared after a year's treatment." One of the doctors went to the extent of making a statement saying that some persons claiming to represent the Roman Catholic Church and the Missionaries of Charity are trying to pressurise him to pass off the case as an inexplicable medical phenomenon. Dr Manzur Murshed, Superintendent of the Balurghat Hospital in South Dinajpur district of West Bengal, said, "They want us to say Monica Besra's recovery was a miracle and beyond the comprehension of medical science." "We advised her a prolonged anti-tubercular treatment, which she followed and was cured," said Tapan Biswas, another doctor who was part of the team that treated Besra. Dr Biswas added, "With all due respect to Mother Teresa, there should not be any talk of a miracle by her."

The West Bengal government ordered an inquiry into this case which was headed by South Dinajpur Additional District Magistrate Goutam Ghosh. Arun Sarkar, an official of the Harirampur block, interviewed villagers, doctors and members of the Besra family before concluding that any talk of a miracle in the woman's cure was baseless. "Monica Besra's tumor was cured purely by medical science. She received continuous anti-tubercular treatment and went through all the necessary curative processes. So any talk of her case being beyond the comprehension of medical science is baseless," Ghosh told reporters on saturday.

Point-counterpoint, the debate seemed complex with each side trying to provide witnesses, testimonies and evidence to prove a point. Sandip Roy, an Indian immigrant in America, recalling his meeting with Mother Teresa said that 'she was miraculous in her utter ordinariness'(*Pacific News Service*-October 21, 2003)

'It is hard to reconcile the images of the giant portrait of Mother Teresa unveiled on the façade of St. Peter's Basilica in Vatican City with the shrunken old lady I saw in Calcutta in the 1970s and '80s. It is harder still to comprehend that someone I actually met would become a saint in my lifetime. Still, as the Vatican scours the world for the miracles that will elevate her to sainthood, it seems to me they are looking in the wrong places.

As students at a Jesuit missionary-run school in Calcutta, we were taken on school outings to the orphanages and 'Home for the Dying' run by the sisters of the Missionaries of Charity. Though we came from all different faiths, every week we all contributed at least 25 paisa (now worth less than a cent) to the 'poor box' that was distributed to charity.

Every now and then we'd be taken to the homes run by the Sisters, to distribute blankets and fruits and evaporated milk bought with the money we'd collected. In a spurt of competitive charity, we'd beg our parents to give us clothes and toys we could give to the kids we would meet.

We would see Mother Teresa occasionally. This was before her 1979 Nobel Prize, and she was not yet quite such a jet-setting nun. She always looked the same – small and wrinkled, impossibly old to our schoolboy eyes, a tiny crumpled figure in her trademark white sari with blue borders. I have no recollection of what she said to us when she would thank us for our donations and then rush off to minister to someone.

I do remember feeling awe-struck that someone would spend her whole life tending to orphans and the sick and dying. This was a world far-removed from our sanitized, upper middle class homes. Here, a drooling, mentally retarded woman beamed at the Mother and grabbed the hem of her sari. We listened enraptured to stories about the 'wild woman' who, rumor had it, had been raised by wolves, or was it bears, before she came to the orphanage. The 'wild woman' never spoke, preferring to slyly cadge cigarettes off the priests who accompanied us. But most of all, we stared at the kids, some our age, rickety and snot-nosed, some deformed, as they clutched our old clothes and toys.

One of the miracles of Mother Teresa was that she allowed the poverty and disease that swirled around us to actually come and touch our insulated lives. Many of us went to school in chauffeur-driven cars, the windows rolled up against the pleadings of limbless beggars at intersections. Those visits to Mother Teresa's institutions were a quick dose of the reality of our own country.

We were the generation born well after India's independence. We had not endured any of the sacrifices of our parents and grandparents, who went to jail for their beliefs or learning to boycott British goods. We grew up with independence as our birthright, sheltered by our parents and fixated on high-paying professions like engineering and surgery.

It took an Albanian nun to help us remember our roots. As an immigrant in the United States today, still holding on to my Indian citizenship, I marvel at the apparent ease with which she gave up her old life and turned herself into an Indian. While immigrants often want the best of both worlds, Mother Teresa took into the folds of her simple sari the castoffs of her adopted country, the people who embarrassed us, whose images were bad PR for a resurgent India.

Of course, there were controversies. She was accused of encouraging death-bed conversions to Catholicism, of consorting with dictators for hefty donations and of being more interested in peaceful deaths than modern medicines. She was fiercely conservative on issues like contraception and sex. I doubt we could have agreed on much if we had actually sat down to a conversation.

But I always remembered the story of the Hindu priests of the Kalighat temple in Calcutta who were incensed when she set up a home for the dying at their doorstep. They feared she was stealing the souls of the dying who came to the temple. But their attitude changed when, at great risk to her own health, she picked up the cholera-stricken son of a Kalighat priest off the streets. When she herself died in 1997, the Kalighat shops downed their shutters in respect.

The Vatican needs one more miracle to make Mother Teresa a full-fledged saint. Their researchers look for cancer cures and disappearing tumors. Now she will be packaged and sold as amulets and postcards. But to me, she will always be the smiling '25 paisa poor box' saint, miraculous in her utter ordinariness.'

Sandip Roy is host of 'Upfront' – the Pacific News Service weekly radio program on KALW-FM, San Francisco.

The Catholic Church grants sainthood to a person only after death. The process requires three authenticated, physical miracles to be performed by the candidate. In Mother Teresa's case, these were miraculous cures that, according to the general belief, occurred due to her divine intervention. Besra's case is well-known. Her malignant stomach tumor disappeared through the agency of a locket bearing Mother Teresa's photograph. Another was a French woman in the United States who broke several ribs in a traffic accident, and who was miraculously made whole because she wore a medallion of Mother Teresa around her neck. A third was a Palestinian girl suffering from cancer who was cured after Mother Teresa appeared to her in a dream and said: "Young girl, you are cured."

The first British case considered in the campaign to make a former nun a saint was the claim by Dr Chandy who was trying to treat one of his patients of severe mental illness. Dr Chandy made his claim in a letter to Sister Nirmala, Mother Teresa's successor as head of the Calcutta mission, which was passed on to the Vatican. The claim stated that Mother Teresa performed a miracle to cure Mr Imms, 54, of manic depression and schizophrenia (reported by Julia Stuart in *The Independent*-London).

Another miracle that is still in evidence relates to a documentary film made by the BBC in the 1960's. Something unusual happened while the crew was filming the interior of the Home of the Dying in Calcutta. Malcolm Muggeridge, in his book '*Something Beautiful for God*, has described the event: 'The interior of the hall was very dark with only one small window and the film crew was not equipped with lights.

The very experienced BBC cameraman was quite adamant that nothing would come out, but because of Mother Teresa's insistence went through the motions of filming. When processed it was found that: 'The film was suffused with a particularly beautiful soft light.' Muggeridge wrote that The House of the Dying is overflowing with love, and this love is luminous, like the haloes that artists paint on saints. The luminosity that is registered on the film, everyone agreed, is quite extraordinarily lovely. The same batch of film was subsequently tested under similar circumstances elsewhere and produced images that were dark and completely useless. Furthermore, back-up footage that was shot for the Mother Teresa documentary outside the Home of the Dying, turned out to be blurred and unusable.'

This incidence did not get much attention from the Roman Catholic Church in the USA and they did not seem very much interested in hearing about the miracles performed by Mother Teresa at that point of time.

On October 1, the Vatican certified that Mother Teresa, who passed away in 1997, had miraculously cured a tribal woman's cancerous tumor in 1998. To be beatified, it is a prerequisite that the person must have performed a miracle from beyond the grave. A potentially miraculous cure must be sudden, permanent and beyond scientific explanation. Pope John Paul II, incidentally, has canonized 464 saints, more than all his predecessors in the last four centuries combined. Besra's cure was claimed as a miracle and Mother Teresa's first posthumous act of healing. This was cited at a ceremony in October 2003 in which the Albanian-born nun was beatified by the Vatican.

More than a decade later, during the commemoration of the tenth anniversary of Mother Teresa's death, Besra complained of being abandoned by the nuns who escorted her to Rome four years ago as the living proof of the miracle performed by their Mother Superior. Her complaint struck a sour note as the crowds gathered in the city for candle lit processions and prayers.

"My hut was frequented by nuns of the Missionaries of Charity before the beatification of Mother Teresa," said Mrs Besra, squatting on the floor of her thatched and mud house in the village of Dangram, 460 miles northeast of Calcutta. "They made of lot of promises to me and assured me of financial help for my livelihood and my children's education... After that, they forgot me. I am living in penury. My husband is sick. My children have stopped going to school as I have no money. I have to work in the fields to feed my husband and five children."

At Mother House, the global headquarters of the Missionaries of Charity which now manages hundreds of homes for the destitute around the world, news of Mrs Besra's complaints were a matter of serious concern. Sister Nirmala, Mother Teresa's successor as superior general, promised to look into her case personally.'Monica Besra herself says she was cured by Mother's miracle. Nuns of the Charity are in touch with Besra. "I talked to her over telephone this morning", she said. "She is upset after her daughter flunked the school-leaving examination this year. We know she is having hard times. We are trying to do our best for her."

Besra says that her own faith in Mother Teresa remained unshaken despite the voices of doubters and her own straightened financial circumstances. 'I find peace when I close my eyes and think of her. I often see her in my dreams,' she said.

Many Indians credit Mother Teresa, a Nobel Laureate, with lighting up their lives with goodness. Her order, the Missionaries of Charity, still looks after thousands of abandoned children and lepers. No matter what her critics say, many Indians have already passed judgment on Mother Teresa. They believe she is one of the greatest Indians ever.

Chapter 14
Spiritual Journey: Canonization / Beatification

The Press Release Of The Postulator Of The Cause Of Beatification And Canonization Of Mother Teresa, dated December 20, 2002, had details of the decrees to be approved by the Pope on heroic virtues and miracles. These included those concerning Mother Teresa. This process is undertaken by the Pope twice a year, before Christmas and in July. Shortly after the approval of the decrees, an announcement regarding the date and place of Mother Teresa's beatification was expected.

Canonization is a process by which a Catholic Church or group declares a deceased person to be a saint and is included in the canon, or list of recognized saints. Originally, individuals were recognized as saints without any formal process. A saint is a disciple of Jesus Christ who spent a lifetime of 'extraordinary fidelity to the Lord, doing God's will in unity with Jesus.' They devoted themselves to the glory of God and are shining examples of all virtues that the human civilization can think of and are introduced to the world as intercessors with God.

The term canonization, also referred to as 'raised to the alters' means assigning of a feast day in the yearly schedule of the Church's liturgical celebrations at the time of beatification which is a step in the process of canonization. By it the Pope allows public veneration of the person in the local Church, within the religious congregation with which he or she was associated, and in other places by those who receive such permission. A saint should be honored in liturgical celebrations by the universal, that is, the whole Church, whereas a 'Blessed' may be so honored in certain places. The aim of the work before beatification is to establish as accurately as possible the historic facts of the candidate's life, to demonstrate the way the candidate practiced the Christian virtues, and to show that the members of the Church, that is, 'the faithful,' consider him or her to be holy and, therefore, worthy of veneration.

This is a complex process involving the Diocesan Phase followed by the Roman Phase. In the Diocesan Phase, the focus is on gathering information through documents and interviews of witnesses under the authority of the local Bishop who is assisted by a Postulator. In Mother Teresa's case, the responsibility was assigned to the Archdiocese of Calcutta. The opening of the Diocesan Phase declares the person concerned as a 'Servant of God.' The second stage, which is the Roman Phase, the findings of the local Church are transferred to the Congregation for the Causes of Saints (CCS), an office of the Vatican, for study and evaluation. This work is done by the Postulator under the supervision of an official of the CCS. After study by a panel of theologians and a commission of cardinals and bishops, the CCS presents its findings to the Pope for his judgment. Finally, the Pope affirms that the Servant of God indeed lived a heroic Christian life; he or she is then called the 'Venerable Servant of God.' The beatification ceremony is held upon the approval of a miracle attributed to the person's intercession.

A miracle is a scientifically inexplicable extraordinary event which is directly attributable to the intercession of the Servant of God. The miracles investigated usually involve cures since they can be easily documented. These miracles, which are subject to a thorough scientific investigation, prove that God Himself is the origin of the person's holiness and he/she is worthy of being canonized. This is an honor conferred upon those by the Church who lived their lives in complete faith by accepting the power of the Holy Spirit within them.

The first persons to be honored by the Christian Church were the Martyrs – those who died for the faith and their sacrifice was considered supreme and undeniable witness to their faith in Christ. It was around the fourth century that 'confessors' – those who had been firm in their faith in life, not in death came to be publicly venerated. Their tombs like those of St. Martin of Tours and St. Hilary of Poitiers were publicly honored and their names were included in the list of saints.

Since its inception, the process of canonization required the approval from the Church. St. Cyprian recommended that utmost diligence ought to be observed while investigating the claims of even martyrs. In fact, according to hearsay, a Catholic matron at Carthage, named Lucilla incurred the wrath of the Church for having kissed the remains of a reputed martyr whose claims remained unproven. The circumstances surrounding the event were scrutinized to prevent undeserving people from recognition. Acts of formal recognition, such as the erection of an alter over the tomb or transferring of the saint's relics to a church were undertaken only after the successful completion of formal inquiries. In the Catholic Church, the process of canonization can be undertaken by the Holy See, which is the administrative division governed by the Pope of the Catholic Church in Rome. Diplomatically and in all spheres the Holy See speaks for the whole Catholic Church and is recognized by the international community as a sovereign entity. When The Church recognizes the sanctity of a person, it implies that they may be publicly invoked and find official mention in the liturgy of the Church. Veneration at the local level requires only beatification, not canonization. The stages of canonization in the Catholic Church are – Servant of God, Venerable, Blessed and finally Sainthood.

To ensure an authoritative decision, the intervention of The Holy See was sought in medieval times on the issue of canonizations. The first instance of a canonization of a saint from outside Rome by the papacy was of St. Udalric Bishop of Augsburg in the tenure of Pope John XV. Walter of Pontoise was the last saint in western Europe to be canonized by an authority other than the pope. Localized venerations were banned with the pope issuing clear decrees that even if miracles are worked through an individual, it is unlawful to venerate him as a saint without the authorization from the Catholic Church.

Stepping into the twentieth century, the papacy continued with simplification of procedures at the diocesan level, initiated by Pope Paul VI, particularly eliminating the office of the Promoter of the Faith, called the Devil's advocate in common parlance. With this, the requirement to present a case against canonization ended, giving impetus to the rate of canonization after 1983.

Sometime during the process, permission is also granted for the body of the Servant of God to be exhumed and examined, a certification ('non cultus') is made that no superstitious or heretical worship or improper cult has grown up around the servant or his or her tomb, and relics are taken. Certain negativity has been attached to the term 'cultus' in modern times, contrary to its meaning in Latin, implying the religious worship of God or a God. When the Church uses this term, it has a specific theological meaning, distinguishing between various forms of worship, the principle being that we must show respect and veneration in proper measure to people who are part of God's plan.

The glorification of saints in the Orthodox Church differs from Roman Catholic tradition in both theology and practice. The glorification of saints is considered to be an act of God, not a declaration of the hierarchy. The official recognition of saints grows from the consensus of the church. The belief is that God may or may not choose to glorify the individual by performance of miracles. Formal investigation is involved to ensure that the individual has been orthodox in faith and the miracles reported are authentic. The glorification service does not 'make' the individual a saint; rather, the Church is simply making a formal acknowledgement of what God has already manifested. In case of martyrs, no formal glorification is required.

Timothy Ware (Bishop Kallistos of Diokleia) has written about canonization in Orthodoxy: 'In private an Orthodox Christian is free to ask for the prayers of any member of the Church, whether canonized or not. It would be perfectly normal for an orthodox child, if orphaned, to end his evening prayers by asking for the intercession not only of the Mother of God and the saints, but of his own mother and father. In its public worship, however, the Church usually asks the prayers only of those whom it has officially proclaimed as saints; but in exceptional circumstances a public cult may become established without any formal act of canonization.' Although the Orthodox Church has recognized Western saints prior to the year 1054, it has not glorified Roman Catholic saints past that year.

National Anglican churches have their own calendars of saints (The calendar of saints is a traditional Christian method of organizing a liturgical year by associating each day with one or more saints and referring to the feast day of said saint). Since the English Reformation, only King Charles I has been canonized in the Church of England. More recently people like C.S.Lewis and Martin Luther King. Jr. have been added to certain Anglican national calendars for commemoration. Lutherans have a calendar of saints, much of which is inherited from the Catholic Church, limiting the recognition of saints to those persons mentioned in the Gospels and the Book of Acts.

Why does the church undertake an enigmatic act of beatifying and canonizing? According to the testimony of Sacred Scriptures every Christian is a saint. The Greek New Testament speaking of Hagios; the Latin Vulgate of the Sancti (saints or holy ones), all of them acknowledge the presence of sacred in all human beings. St. Peter, addressing the Christian community said, 'You are a chosen race, a royal priesthood, a holy nation, a people of his own, so that you may announce the praises of him who called you out of darkness into His wonderful light.' In a technical and stricter sense, saints are those people in whose lives Christ's victory over sin, the devil and death has been completed. It is the call for perfection, goodness and holiness. Nothing imperfect ever enters into heaven, therefore, Christ called us to 'be perfect as our heavenly Father.' Those who do not follow the prescribed path would enter the purifying fires and made perfect. Perfection was conformity to Christ in his death and relics of people who devoted their lives in this faith were preserved and guarded. The honors bestowed upon them are illustrated in The Circular Letter of the Church of Smyrna on the Martyrdom of St. Polycarp in 155 AD: 'We have at last gathered his bones, which are dearer to us than priceless gems and purer than gold, and laid them to rest where it was befitting they should lie. And if it be possible for us to assemble again, may God grant us to celebrate the birthday of his martyrdom with gladness, thus to recall the memory of those who fought in the glorious combat, and to teach and strengthen by his example those who shall come after us.' The greatest tribute to a martyr was to have his or her name mentioned in the canon of the mass.

Even though the age of martyrs never ended, the church did begin to look for other models of holiness, those whose lives were marked by heroic virtues, signaling the triumph of light over darkness, of grace over sin and Christ over Satan. The centralization of the canonization process in Rome attempts at providing a moral certitude and credibility to the possibility of a person being in heaven.

The celebration of Mother Teresa's beatification at St. Peter's Square was witnessed by a sea of humanity. Missionaries of Charity issued a statement saying that 'We, the Missionaries of Charity, give thanks and praise to God that our Holy Father, Pope John Paul II, has officially recognized the holiness of our mother, Mother Teresa, and approved the miracle obtained through her intercession. We are filled with joy in anticipation of the beatification that will take place in Rome on Mission Sunday, 19 October 2003, the closest Sunday to the twenty-fifth anniversary of the Holy Father's Pontificate and the end of the Year of the Rosary.' She was one step away from sainthood – another miracle was needed to complete the process. Addressing the crowd, Pope John Paul II said, "Brothers and sisters, even in our days God inspires new models of sainthood, some impose themselves for their radicalness, like that offered by Mother Teresa, whom today we add to the ranks of the blessed... In her, we perceive the urgency to put oneself in a state of service, especially for the poorest and most forgotten, the last of the last." During the ceremony, a smiling portrait of Mother Teresa was unveiled and she is henceforth called the Blessed Mother Teresa of Calcutta. The Pope had made an exception for her by reducing the waiting period from five years to two years for awarding sainthood by allowing instant beatification. Members of Mother Teresa's congregation believe that people have experienced God's love for them through her prayers and many pilgrims from around the globe come to pray at her tomb and try to follow her example of service to humanity. After the announcement of her beatification, her message is cherished by people of all faiths. Mother Teresa, even before being canonized by the

Vatican, was commonly known as the 'Saint of the Gutters', a modern day saint around the world. A long time friend of Mother Teresa, Archbishop D'Souza believed that 'God will provide miracle to prove her cause as it was her single mindedness, devotion to humanity as well as consistency in efforts that made the world recognize her hard work.' Mother often said, "Holiness is not the luxury of the few, it is a simple duty for each one of us." May her example help us to strive for holiness: to love God, to respect and love every human person created by God in His own image and in whom He dwells, and to care for our poor and suffering brethren. May all the sick, the suffering, and those who seek God's help find a friend and intercessor in Mother Teresa.'

Father Brian Kolodiejchuk of the Missionaries of Charity, postulator for the sainthood cause of Blessed Teresa of Calcutta, told a gathering at the Knights of Columbus Museum in New Haven on June 1 that her cause is 'still waiting for one more miracle' for her to be declared a saint. He was speaking in New Haven on her life and mission on the occasion of her hundredth birth anniversary. "Someone has to ask Mother Teresa's intercession, then Mother Teresa has to intercede, God has to (perform) the miracle, someone has to report the miracle... and then we can continue with the process," he said of the canonization process. "We get thousands of reports of favors from people praying," he noted, "but so far, nothing that can be presented as a miracle."

Mother Teresa's relics including crucifix, rosary and sandals were displayed at the Basilica of the National Shrine of the Immaculate Conception in Washington. The crucifix was the one she wore from the time of her first vows at the age of twenty till her death. The rosary and sandals were being used at the time of her death. The relics then traveled to St. Patrick's Cathedral in New York, on June 7 to be venerated. On the occasion, Kolodiejchuk said that her legacy will keep reminding us of what it means to be human and how every human being is a child of God created in His image. "She was a woman passionately in love with Jesus," the priest said. "She taught us that the way to our human fulfillment and happiness begins by giving oneself through love put into action through service to others' and by doing 'ordinary things with extraordinary love."

Christopher Hitchens tried all along to demystify the myths surrounding Mother Teresa. He was highly critical of her nomination for beatification immediately after her demise and abolition of the office of the 'devil's advocate', defining the phenomenon as 'abject surrender on the part of the Church to the forces of showbiz, superstition and populism.' Attestation of the miracle is obviously fake with the treating staff giving evidence to the contrary and none of the doctors were interviewed by the Vatican investigators. Even though he was personally interviewed, he continued to insist that consultation with doubters was necessary.

According to an uncontradicted report in the Italian paper *L'Eco di Bergamo,* the Vatican's secretary of state sent a letter to senior cardinals in June, asking on behalf of the Pope whether they favored making Mother Teresa a saint right away. The pope's clear intention has been to speed the process up in order to perform the ceremony in his own lifetime. The response was in the negative, according to Father Brian Kolodiejchuk, the Canadian priest who has acted as postulator or advocate for the 'canonization.' A question mark had been put on the integrity of the whole process.

Hitchens draws reference to the corrupt practices of the medieval church saying that 'it sold indulgences to the rich while preaching hellfire and continence to the poor... Mother Teresa was not a friend of the poor. She was a friend of *poverty*. She said that suffering was a gift from God. She spent her life opposing the only known cure for poverty, which is the empowerment of women and the emancipation of them from a livestock version of compulsory reproduction. And she was a friend to the worst of the rich, taking misappropriated money from the atrocious Duvalier family in Haiti (whose rule she praised in return) and from Charles Keating of the Lincoln Savings and Loan. Where did that money, and all the other donations, go? The primitive hospice in Calcutta was as run down when she died as it always had been—she preferred California clinics when she got sick herself—and her order always refused to publish any audit. But we have her own claim that she opened 500 convents in more than a hundred countries, all bearing the name of her own order. Excuse me, but is this modesty and humility?'

Many people in the rich world, in order to address their own conscience were investing in her acts of charity and a myth was permitted to arise. Quite a few volunteers returned disillusioned by 'the stern ideology and poverty loving practice of the congregation.'

'One of the curses of India, as of other poor countries, is the quack medicine man, who fleeces the sufferer by promises of miraculous healing. Sunday was a great day for these parasites, who saw their crummy methods endorsed by his holiness and given a more or less free ride in the international press. Forgotten were the elementary rules of logic, that extraordinary claims require extraordinary evidence and that what can be asserted without evidence can also be dismissed without evidence. More than that, we witnessed the elevation and consecration of extreme dogmatism, blinkered faith and the cult of a mediocre human personality. Many more people are poor and sick because of the life of Mother Teresa: even more will be poor and sick if her example is followed. She was a fanatic, a fundamentalist and a fraud, and a Church that officially protects those who violate the innocent has given us another clear sign of where it truly stands on moral and ethical questions.'

Mother Teresa, known to champion the cause of the poor and a favourite with the media, wined and dined with the rich and the famous. For many years, she was the most revered woman in the world. 'Mother Teresa's 'hospitals' for the indigent in India and elsewhere turned out to be hardly more than human warehouses in which seriously ill persons lay on mats, sometimes fifty to sixty in a room without benefit of adequate medical attention. Their ailments usually went undiagnosed. The food was nutritionally lacking and sanitary conditions were deplorable. There were few medical personnel on the premises, mostly untrained nuns and brothers. When tending to her own ailments, however, Teresa checked into some of the costliest hospitals and recovery care units in the world for state-of-the-art treatment.'

Her critiques have further accused her of spreading promotional misinformation about herself. The statistics related to her hospices was proved to be false. She claimed that her school in a Calcutta slum had five thousand children when less than one hundred were actually enrolled there. Teresa claimed to have 102 family assistance centers in Calcutta, but longtime Calcutta resident, Aroup Chatterjee, who did an extensive on-the-scene investigation of her mission, could not find a single such center. The inaccuracies in the statistical projections continued and seemed to aim at exaggerating her accomplishments.

Her supporters have been defending her on the grounds that Mother Teresa was never really worried about statistics. The emphasis was always on how much love is put into the work and not how much work is done.

Another criticism leveled against her is that while living a lavish life herself, spending a good part of her life outside Calcutta, travelling in private jets in Europe and America, she continued to glorify poverty. All this seems to go unnoticed. She was speaking with the elite, maintaining cordial relations with people whose credentials were doubtful and did not speak much about social injustices and for progressive reforms.

Her 'Crisis of Faith' was putting hurdles in the way of her canonization in 2007, exposing the contradictions in her life. As the popular belief went, she was a living example of spiritual joy and unshakable faith, but her diary entries revealed information to the contrary. She was full of doubts about her own faith and existence of God for many decades. People think 'my faith, my hope and my love are overflowing and that my intimacy with God and union with his will fill my heart. If only they knew,' she wrote, 'Heaven means nothing.'

Sainthood, many believe, an institution of the Church, was used by Pope John Paul for his political agenda. Ultra-conservatives were sanctified with the likes of Mother Teresa and the last of the Hapsburg rulers of the Austro-Hungarian Empire, Emperor Karl. Another reactionary set up for sainthood was Pius IX, who reigned as pontiff from 1846 to 1878 and is infamous for referring to Jews as 'dogs.' John Paul also beatified Cardinal Aloysius Stepinac, the leading Croatian cleric who welcomed the Nazi and fascist Ustashi takeover of Croatia during World War II. Stepinac sat in the Ustashi parliament, appeared at numerous public events with top ranking Nazis and Ustashi, and openly supported the Croatian fascist regime that exterminated hundreds of thousands of Serbs, Jews and Romans ('gypsies').

Chapter 15
Media—Image Building

Mother Teresa, a missionary, a saint, someone who spoke of peace, love and service to humanity was the most revered woman in the world for quite some time and of course, the focus of media attention. Her life became a source of inspiration and she managed to move many hearts to the cause of the poor, the sick and the needy. Media played a very important role in spreading her message across the globe. This section contains excerpts from media coverage of Mother Teresa which, most would agree was instrumental in transforming her acts from local charity to a global mission.

Her popularity continued to rise with the increase in the membership of her congregation and expansion of hospices. From her works of charity to her crisis of faith, from controversial views on sensitive issues to sainthood – everything seemed to be making news. *New York Times,* reported in 2007, 'Two new entries climb to the top of the hard cover nonfiction list: Bill Clinton's *'Giving'* and a dark book of letters from Mother Teresa called *'Mother Teresa: Come Be My Light.'*

Time magazine published an extensive interview by Edward W. Desmond, titled: *A Pencil in the Hand of God;*

Mother Teresa sees poverty as a kind of richness, and richness as impoverishment – as she cares for the dying and unwanted of Calcutta, covering various facets of her life and her work. Her day began with prayers, and the same interface with the divine was translated into service and everyone including volunteers were given a chance to touch the poor. 'Everybody has to experience that. So many young people give up everything to do just that. This is something so completely unbelievable in the world, no? And yet it is wonderful. Our volunteers go back different people.'

When asked to comment on the criticism against the severe regimen under which she and her sisters lived, she replied, "We choose that. That is the difference between us and the poor. Because that will bring us closer to our poor people. How can we be truthful to them if we lead a different life? What language will I speak to them?" Mother Teresa presented the Gospel without the gloss. She said that the most joyful place she had ever visited was Kalighat. "When the people die in peace, in the love of God, it is a wonderful thing. To see our poor people happy together with their families, these are beautiful things. The joy of the poor people is so clean, so clear. The real poor know what is joy." The future of the order, Mother Teresa believed was in God's hands – Human beings only have to take care of the present.

Some of her letters which were preserved against her wish and later published in the form of a book, revealing how she experienced doubts over her own faith, shook the world and suddenly the headlines changed from 'A Living Saint' to 'A Saint of Darkness.' People were startled to discover that hers was a dispirited life, littered with doubts. A new book of her letters, *'Mother Teresa: Come Be My Light,'* published by Doubleday, showed her struggling for decades against disbelief. 'If I ever become a saint,' she wrote in one letter, 'I will surely be one of 'darkness'. And in another: 'If there be no God—there can be no soul. If there is no soul then Jesus—You also are not true. Heaven, what emptiness.'

'I think there is no suffering greater than what is caused by the doubts of those who want to believe,' wrote Flannery O'Connor, the Roman Catholic author whose stories traverse the landscape of twentieth century unbelief. 'What people don't realize is how much religion costs. They think faith is a big electric blanket, when of course it is the cross. It is much harder to believe than not to believe.' O'Connor suffered from isolation and devastating illness, Mother Teresa from decades of spiritual emptiness. Despite the pain caused by the longing for a sense of the divine, Mother Teresa kept faith with the sick of Calcutta.

The saga that was Mother Teresa is apparent from the accounts of people whose lives were touched by her. Ashish Chakrabarti, writing in *Indian Express* in 1998, narrated the story of a boy.

Sixteen year old Sunil Das used to work in a roadside eating place at Halisahar, about 50 km north of Calcutta. About a month ago, when his legs showed symptoms of leprosy, his employer sent him home. But the boy's stepmother would not keep him with the family and his father, a construction worker, pleaded helplessness. He was brought to the Gandhiji Prem Nivas, a center for leprosy patients run by the Missionaries of Charity at Titagarh. Last

Tuesday, Sunil was to be released as his legs had improved but he pleaded with Brother Eugene, the man in charge of the center, to let him stay in the adjoining hostel… "I won't go back home because my stepmother never loved me. Now that I had this disease, they won't take me back. I'm much better here." Sunil who never went to school had not heard of Mother Teresa until last August 26 when they observed the late nun's eighty eighth birth anniversary at the center. "We were told she loved people like us, the poor and the sick, whom nobody loved and cared for."

Mother Teresa's demise created a vacuum in the city of Calcutta – something that no one was able to fill up. Her presence was overpowering and the people whom she worked for and lived with actually felt abandoned. Chitrita Banerjee, recalled how she was asked by one of her colleagues on return from her hometown, Calcutta, "Welcome back. And how is everyone in Calcutta—still starving and being looked after by Mother Teresa?" This is how it was – the only images that were evoked in the West when it came to Calcutta were those suffering masses of humanity being tended by Mother Teresa.

Mother Teresa's demise saw foreign dignitaries and the western news media descend on the city. 'The reports on the funeral portrayed a city filled with starving orphans, wretched slums and dying people abandoned on the streets, except for the fortunate ones rescued by Mother Teresa. They described a city I didn't recognize as the place where I had spent the first twenty years of my life.'

'The answer was that none of them served for seven decades as the adopted home base for a saintly European crusader whose work could succeed only if it was disproportionately magnified. It was an instance of spin in which the news media colluded—voluntarily or not—with a religious figure who was as shrewd as any fund-raising politician, as is evident from the global expansion of her organization. For Calcutta natives like me, however, Mother Teresa's charity also evoked the colonial past—she felt she knew what was best for the Third World masses, whether it was condemning abortion or offering to convert those who were on the verge of death.' Even after so many years, the news media continues to portray Calcutta in the same light and her organization fervently projects her as an icon of mercy. 'Charity need not be inconsistent with clarity. Calcutta is a modern Indian city where poverty and inequality co-exist with measurably increasing prosperity, expanding opportunities, cautious optimism and above all, pride in its unique character. Mother Teresa might have meant well, but she furthered her mission by robbing Calcutta of its richly nuanced identity while pretending to love it.'

The euphoria, the adulation, desperate search for a miracle and road to sainthood marked Mother Teresa's life and death. 'The wonder of the miracle is due to the fact that its cause is hidden, and an effect is expected other than what actually takes place,' the Catholic Encyclopedia explains. "Saints are examples rather than miracle workers or intercessors," says the Reverand Richard P. Mc Brien, author of *Lives of the Saints'* (Harper Collins, 2001). 'They are signs of what it means to be human in the fullest and best sense of the word. Which is also why the church has been wrong to have canonized so many priests and nuns rather than married lay people who lived ordinary lives in extraordinary ways, rejoicing in their children and grandchildren and doing good for so many others?'

The miracle was ultimately identified in the healing of malignant tumor of a Bengali tribal woman and the beatification of Mother Teresa began. Fr. Sebastian Vazhakala, co-founder of the male Missionaries of Charity and one of the more than a hundred witnesses, having worked with Mother Teresa for thirty two years, said, "Without pressuring anyone, her life was an invitation to others; she involved them in a life of prayer and service." Reuters, covering the event in Rome, reported:

'An ailing Pope John Paul beatified Mother Teresa before a crowd of 300,000 on Sunday, calling her an icon of charity and launching her on the fast track to sainthood. The two-and-a-half-hour ceremony in St. Peter's square was a multi-colored, multi-lingual service that reflected Mother Teresa's global appeal. There were Indian girls dancing with incense and flowers, hundreds of Mother Teresa's nuns dressed in white and blue saris, cardinals in red silk, presidents in blue suits and Rome's homeless wearing hand-outs from shelters. On the altar before Christendom's largest church, the Pope managed to read the formula of beatification with difficulty in Latin. Applause and cheering broke out in the vast crowd when a giant tapestry showing a smiling Mother Teresa was unveiled. "I am personally grateful to this courageous woman, who I always felt was at my side," the Pope said of Mother Teresa of Calcutta in his homily. "She was an icon of the Good Samaritan," he added. "She had chosen to be not just the least but to be the servant of the least." The Pope praised Mother Teresa, who died in 1997 aged eighty seven, for 'her faith-filled conviction that, in touching the broken bodies of the poor, she was touching the body of Christ.' A MULTI-FAITH FOLLOWING Catholic and non-Catholic admirers packed the square and filled the broad Via della Conciliazione from the Vatican to the River Tiber... In the crowd were the presidents of Albania and Macedonia, Alfred Moisiu and Boris Trajkovski, former Polish President Lech Walesa, Bernadette Chirac, wife of the French president, French Prime Minister Jean-Pierre Raffarin and many Italian leaders.'

The acceleration of the process of beatification raised many questions about the motives behind making this exception. The prefect of the Congregation disclosed that there were very particular motives, 'as the spread of the fame of sanctity which Mother Teresa enjoys universally, both within and outside the Church.' Moreover, the Archbishop referred to the 'extraordinary ecclesial relevance which is invested in the figure of the founder of the Missionaries of Charity.' And finally, to 'the avalanche of petitions which have come from very varied sources in the Catholic Church, as well as groups and individuals or institutions which are not part of the Church.' In India, considering the consensus between all religious groups on the issue, many feel that this honor by the Church for the founder of the Missionaries of Charity, could act as a bridge between Catholics, Hindus and Muslims.

Archbishop D'Souza recounting one of the encounters said, "Last year I visited the Holy Land. In Galilee, at Cana, a Palestinian woman stopped me and said: 'You must be the Archbishop of Calcutta. I have a photograph of you and Mother Teresa.' She went on to tell me about her granddaughter who had been gravely ill with bone cancer,' the Archbishop recounted to 'Fides.' 'The night before the little girl was to be operated on, she had a dream: a woman in a white dress trimmed with blue said to her: 'Have no fear, you are cured.' The little girl had no idea who the woman of the dream could be. The next day, as the doctors were about to begin the operation, they saw the disease had disappeared. After the miraculous cure, the little girl's family tried to identify the lady of the dream and they discovered it was Mother Teresa,' the Archbishop said to 'Fides.'

But devotion to Mother Teresa is spreading even without miracles. "Her life of love dedicated to the poorest of the poor is the most beautiful sign of God's presence among us," the Archbishop said. Even when she was alive, 'Mother' was treated like a saint by Christians, Hindus and Moslims. People knelt to kiss her feet – a typical Hindu sign of respect – or touch her sari. 'Mother Teresa's burial place, at the Calcutta home of the Missionaries, has been a site of pilgrimage since the hour of her death. Hundreds visit every day: school groups, individuals and people from India and from all over the world. People venerate her pictures and she is constantly invoked, particularly by the poorest. The Archbishop continues to receive reports of miracles and requests for prayers. "Only yesterday, I had a letter from a woman in Bombay asking me to pray to Mother Teresa to obtain a special grace. No one organizes this movement; it is all quite spontaneous."

Her life and her teachings had an impact on international issues of vital importance – the troubles that the world is grappling with. Search for peace, call for disarmament – all these efforts could gain momentum if one were to draw lessons from Mother Teresa's life. Speaking on the occasion of her first death anniversary, Pope spoke in remembrance of Mother

Teresa—"Let us not forget the great example left by Mother Teresa, and let us not limit ourselves by commemorating her with words! May we have the courage to always put the person first and their fundamental rights. To the heads of nations, be they rich or poor, I say: do not put your trust in the power of arms! Proceed decisively and faithfully on the path of disarmament, so as to destine necessary resources to the true, main objectives of civilization, to combat in unity against hunger and sickness, so that every person may live and die with dignity. God himself wants this, and reminds us of it also through the testimony of Mother Teresa. 'May she help and accompany us to Heaven!'

The 1979 Nobel Peace Prize winner traveled around the world with the frequency of a diplomatic crisis-solver and was often mobbed by her admirers with the kind of enthusiasm reserved for rock stars or royalty. Even as she met and interacted with the rich and the powerful, Mother Teresa never shifted her priorities and her commitment to be with the poorest of the poor. Her official biographer, Navin Chawla said, "People, particularly the poor, responded to her kindness, her compassion and the fact that this single woman would reach out to them when no one else would... She reached out to destitution everywhere, no matter where they were, from AIDS patients in Los Angeles to the poor who lived under the London Bridge."

Carrying on with the tasks in the absence of Mother Teresa seems to be a Herculean task and media has been carrying stories about lapses in the dispensing of duties on part of her congregation. A story unfolded barely three months after her death before a crowd outside Nirmal Hriday (The Pure Heart), the home for the sick and dying adjoining the famous Kali temple at Kalighat. An old ragpicker woman lay huddled on a nearby sidewalk, her frail body racked by fever and exhaustion, while her beggar husband knocked on the doors of the Missionaries home for medicine and shelter. But the doors remained shut. It would not happened in Mother's time, exclaimed a neighborhood shop owner.

"It was a mistake," admits Sister Nirmala who succeeded Mother Teresa as Superior General of the order, "it happened because the sister in charge of the home was away. But the woman was later taken in and she died peacefully with us." Sister Luke, a Singapore-domiciled Malayalee who has been with the home for twenty years, confirmed the incident adding. 'Such things happened even when Mother was there because there are always far more people wanting to come in than we can accommodate. We've to move out people who get better to make room for the more needy."

Growing expectations of the people and infrastructural problems faced by the congregation are leading to dissatisfaction. Fr. Camille Bouche, who has been a spiritual advisor to the order, is worried even while acknowledging the good work done by the brothers and the sisters. Another reason behind this has been the declining number of girls joining the order due to the changing family patterns in Kerala from where majority of sisters and brothers had come over the past decades. 'People with one daughter do not wish to give the child to the church anymore.'

Sister Nirmala, speaking to *The Indian Express* on life at the Missionaries after Mother Teresa said: "We miss Mother. Although her body is here (at Mother House tomb), we miss her physical presence. She's changed address from earth to heaven. But her spirit is here with us and in our homes... It's going on as before, as Mother wanted. Since her death,

ninteen new houses have been sanctioned all over the world…
The volunteers keep coming in large numbers. It's God's
work." When asked about Mother Teresa's contribution, she
replied, "She never claimed to wipe off poverty or sickness.
She tried to wipe off the tears, reduce the pain and bring
hope for the poor and the sick. She made a difference as she
created awareness about such poor people." Mother Teresa's
remains are in India but the Albanian government has asked
India to return them to her native country by the hundredth
anniversary of her birth. BBC carried the story of India's
rejection of this demand.

"Mother Teresa was an Indian citizen and she is resting
in her own country, her own land," Foreign Ministry
spokesman Vishnu Prakash said. A spokeswoman for the
nun's Missionaries of Charity described the Albanian request
as 'absurd'. Correspondents say that the row over her resting
place could develop into an ugly three-way squabble between
India, where she worked most of her life, Albania where her
parents came from and Macedonia where she lived the first
eighteen years of her life. The row is expected to intensify
by August next year – the hundredth anniversary of Mother
Teresa's birth – by which time many commentators expect
her to have been canonised as a saint. After her death in
September 1997, Mother Teresa was buried at the Calcutta
headquarters of the Missionaries of Charity (MoC), which
is now a pilgrimage site. "We welcome Delhi's decision.
Mother Teresa is Calcutta's, she is India's. It is absurd for
Albania to expect her last remains," MoC spokeswoman
Sunita Kumar told the BBC. In comments reported over
the weekend, Albanian Prime Minister Sali Berisha said his
government would intensify efforts to reclaim her remains
before her birth centenary.

Nobel Peace Prize honoree Mother Teresa is one of the legendary figures headlining the 2010 stamp program announced by the US Postal Service. The stamp features a portrait of Mother Teresa painted by award-winning artist Thomas Blackshear. This is in recognition of her exemplary service to humanity. She also happened to be an honorary US citizen, which was awarded to her by President Bill Clinton and the US Congress in 1996. 'Her humility and compassion, as well as her respect for the innate worth and dignity of humankind, inspired people of all ages and backgrounds to work on behalf of the world's poorest populations.' Before this, she was honored with the Presidential Medal of Freedom in 1985 by President Ronald Reagan when she started working on behalf of AIDS sufferers in the US.

Mixed signals have been coming from the US. On the one hand the government honored her with a stamp, on the other hand the empire state building refused to light up for Mother Teresa. When the 102 storied building lights up the Manhattan sky, the colors convey a meaning – a holiday or may be a charitable cause. But this time, these colors are shrouded in the clouds of controversy. Building owner has refused to light it to honor Mother Teresa on her hundredth birthday saying that the privately owned building 'has a specific policy against any other lighting for religious figures or requests by religions and religious organizations.'

The lay advocacy group – Catholic League, which requested the lights for Mother Teresa, countered that individual religious figures have, in fact, been posthumously honored at the Empire State Building: Cardinal John O'Connor in 2000, with the red and white colors of his position; Pope John Paul II in 2005, with the tower lights symbolically extinguished; and famed Baptist preacher

In this September 30, 2009 file photo, the moon rises above New York as the Empire State building is lit in red and yellow in honor of communist China's sixtieth anniversary. Catholics criticized the owners of the landmark skyscraper for declining to illuminate it in honor of the late Mother Teresa, who was to turn 100 on August 26, 2010. - AP Photo

Martin Luther King Jr. with red, black and green. More than 40,000 people have signed a petition in support of the special lights for Mother Teresa. "I don't think this is about religion," City Council Speaker, Quinn said. "Mother Teresa was a nun, obviously, but she was much more than that; she was a Nobel Prize winner... who inspired people of all religions."

In the meantime, *Asia News* reported on May 12, 2010, that the city of Kolkata is busy preparing to celebrate Mother Teresa's centennial. The archdiocese, the Missionaries of Charity and the faithful of the Indian metropolis are planning important celebrations to mark the centennial of the birth of the Blessed. Local Catholics are praying and hoping that the canonization of Mother Teresa will be announced during this anniversary. Celebrations will take place between August 17 and September 13 and the most important event will be the novena for the canonization of the Blessed which will be recited in every parish in the diocese during the centennial period. On August 26, Card Telesphore Toppo will celebrate a Mass in the Mother House and on the same day, a film festival and an exhibition of paintings dedicated to her life will open. A symposium on her life is also is the offing with Navin Chawla, her biographer and Fr. Brian Kolodiejchuk, postulator of her canonization as speakers. The archdiocese has proclaimed September 5, the day she was born in heaven, a day of celebration, which will end in a Mass in the courtyard of Saint Francis Xavier College.

Chapter 16

Mother Teresa and the World Leaders

Mother Teresa had come to exercise a significant and substantial influence in the international scenario. Even though she was not rich and glamorous, royalty and the world leaders interacted with her and welcomed her visits. She enjoyed direct access to them and managed to get attentive hearing. This was the result of tirelessly striving and working for the cause of humanity with extraordinary compassion and complete dedication. She set selfless goals for herself and ventured into areas where most feared to go, focusing on the poorest of the poor, the sick and the malnourished, people who are suffering from ailments like leprosy and AIDS. Accepting the 1979 Nobel Peace Prize, Mother Teresa said, "I choose the poverty of our poor people. But I am grateful to receive (the Nobel) in the name of the hungry, the naked, the homeless, of the crippled, of the blind, of the lepers, of all those people who feel unwanted, unloved, uncared for throughout society, people that have become a burden to the society and are shunned by everyone." She believed in tolerance in the face of hardships and personified the potential goodness of humankind. When it came to serving people, no distinction was made in terms of religion or nationality. Her thoughts and teachings were voluntarily followed by people across the world. She became a role model, inspiring millions to tread her path. As contended by Marshall McLuhan, her medium to convey her message to the world was – her actions, her self-imposed poverty and her lifestyle amidst the slums of the world. To add to this, she was not just a preacher but practiced more than she preached.

Winning international support for the cause was essential but she did not seek the limelight and all the greatness was imposed upon her by the media. Contributions from people came to her congregation from almost all countries – Mother Teresa had the ability to move the hearts and minds of the most powerful in the world. Meetings with the high and mighty focused on the interests of the marginalized. Her global influence was apparent in the presence of foreign dignitaries at the time of her funeral. Mother Teresa's vision and message is beginning to be realized.

Mother Teresa shared a special relationship with Princess Diana. The year 1997 was rather traumatic with two iconic celebrities dying within days of each other. Media in New York speculated that Mother Teresa died of a cardiac arrest since she could not bear the grief of the death of her friend, the Princess of Wales. The two women were so different, living lives which were truly worlds apart and yet having so much in common. When Princess Diana died, Mother Teresa's condolence message read – 'She was very concerned for the poor. She was very anxious to do something for them. That is why she was close to me.' Both spent most of their lives under media gaze. In their loving memory, a stamp has

Stamp released by the Ascension Island, depicting
Mother Teresa and Princess Diana together

been released by the Ascension Island, depicting Mother
Teresa and Princess Diana together. Princess Diana used
her influential status to support charitable causes including
campaign against landmines and speaking for AIDS sufferers.

In 1985, President Ronald Reagan of the United States
of America, gave a speech while awarding The Medal of
Freedom to Mother Teresa. These are the excerpts from his
speech.

'This great house receives many great visitors, but none more special or more revered than our beloved guest today. A month ago, we awarded the Medal of Freedom to thirteen heroes who have done their country proud. Only one of the recipients could not attend because she had work to do – not special work, not unusual work for her, but everyday work which is both special and urgent in its own right. Mother Teresa was busy, as usual, saving the world. And I mean that quite literally. And so we rather appreciated her priorities, and we're very happy, indeed, that she could come to America this week… Some people, some very few people are, in the truest sense, citizens of the world; Mother Teresa is. And we love her so much we asked her to accept our tribute, and she graciously accepted…Mother Teresa is a heroine of our times. And to the many honors she has received, including the Nobel Peace Prize, we add, with deep affection and endless respect, the Presidential Medal of Freedom.'

'And I want to thank you for something, Mother Teresa. Your great work and your life have inspired so many Americans to become personally involved, themselves, in helping the poor. So many men and women in every area of life, in government and the private sector, have been led by the light of your love, and they have given greatly of themselves. And we thank you for your radiant example.'

In her reply, Mother Teresa said, "I am most unworthy of this generous gift of our President, Mr Reagan and his wife, and you people of United States. But I accept it for the greater glory of God and in the name of the millions of poor people that this gift, in spirit and in love, will penetrate the hearts of the people. For in giving it to me, you are giving it to them, to my hands, with your great love and concern.'

Photograph of The Reagans presenting Mother Teresa with the Medal of Freedom at a White House Ceremony (June 20, 1985)

Hillary Clinton, present Secretary of State and former First lady of the United States, fondly remembering Mother Teresa recalled how Mother Teresa compelled her to encourage adoption. Addressing the gathering on the fifty-eighth annual National Prayer Breakfast (event organized by the secretive Washington network, The Family, a group of elite fundamentalists ministering to DC's powerful and wealthy), Hillary Clinton underscored the Family's influence in pushing her stance on reproductive freedom rightward. Clinton recalled meeting Mother Teresa at the 1994 National Prayer Breakfast, a platform used by Mother Teresa to draw reference to the nominal support extended by the Clintons to abortion rights. Mother Teresa spoke of love, of selfishness, of a lack of love for the unborn—and a lack of want of the unborn because of selfishness. After an awkward silence, the entire ballroom erupted in a standing ovation that seemed to last minutes. It felt even longer to the embarrassed Clintons (and Al and Tipper Gore), who remained seated and did not clap.

Hillary managed to turn this public snubbing into a highly visible friendship with the nun. Hillary's reflections and description of the encounter depict certain tense moments:

'In February of 1994, the speaker here was Mother Teresa. She gave, as everyone who remembers that occasion will certainly recall, a strong address against abortion. And then she asked to see me. And I thought, 'Oh, dear.' (Laughter.) And after the breakfast, we went behind that curtain and we sat on folding chairs, and I remember being struck by how small she was and how powerful her hands were, despite her size, and that she was wearing sandals in February in Washington...We began to talk, and she told me that she knew that we had a shared conviction about adoption being vastly better as a choice for unplanned or unwanted babies. And she asked me—or more properly, she directed me—to work with her to create a home for such babies here in Washington. I know that we often picture, as we're growing up, God as a man with a white beard. But that day, I felt like I had been ordered, and that the message was coming not just through this diminutive woman but from someplace far beyond.'

Mother Teresa, with her physical frailty and spiritual and rhetoric strength left an indelible mark on this distinguished gathering of around 3000 people, including the president, vice president, their spouses and the congressional leaders, cutting to the heart of the social ills afflicting America. After the 1994 Breakfast, Mother Teresa insisted Clinton prove her dedication to abortion alternatives by setting up an orphanage for the nun in Washington DC. In her autobiography, Clinton writes that Mother Teresa was a 'relentless lobbyist,' pushing Hillary to follow through on her promise to get Mother Teresa 'her center for babies.' The Mother Teresa Home for Infant Children opened in 1995. On opening day, writes Clinton, Mother Teresa 'gripped my arm in her small, strong hand and dragged me upstairs to see the freshly painted nursery and rows of bassinets waiting to be filled with infants. Her enthusiasm was irresistible. By then I fully understood how this humble nun could move nations to her will.' Now, the building that had housed the orphanage (on Western Avenue in the affluent neighborhood of Chevy Chase, in DC) has been put up for sale and is being advertised as ideal embassy location in one the most affluent neighborhoods in the country.

Hillary Clinton, Mother Teresa, and the DC house, since sold, that was intended for an orphanage

With the Vatican and the Pope, Mother Teresa continued to share a very special relationship since she was believed to be doing God's work on earth. In 1971, Paul VI awarded her the first Pope John XXIII Peace Prize and eventual beatification by the Holy See. Some of her critics alleged that Mother Teresa held on to pre-Vactian III belief that salvation is only possible through the Roman Catholic Church. Her Vatican biography says, 'The whole of Mother Teresa's life and labor bore witness to the joy of loving, the greatness and dignity of every human person, the value of little things done faithfully and with love, and the surpassing worth of friendship with God.'

27 June 1997: Popev John Paul II blesses Mother Teresa at the Vatican City

Chapter 17
The Myth Lives On

To scrutinize Mother Teresa's life is indeed an arduous task mainly because the aura surrounding her image would deter anyone from critically analyzing her belief system and her works of charity. How many of us, in any case are capable of sacrificing a lifetime for a selfless cause. Mother Teresa was definitely an extraordinary person and the criticisms leveled against her can in no way downplay her global contribution. Now that she is no more, she cannot defend herself against the aspersions that have been cast upon her and the Missionaries of Charity – not that she was particularly interested in doing so while she was alive.

Media continued to glorify her, starting from Malcolm Muggeridge's documentary in 1969 and later, his book *Something Beautiful for God: Mother Teresa of Calcutta.* International media has played a vital role in shifting her from the pages of history to the realm of myth. Noted anthropologist Claude Levi Strauss, along with writers Lapierre and Muggeridge had already projected Calcutta as a city of poverty, oppressed by its own population. The plight of the city, they maintained, had nothing to do with exploitation or was not a result of western imperialism.

Therefore, the answer was not to be found in waging a war against capitalism but in saints like Mother Teresa.

Whether Mother Teresa was part of a global enterprise for alleviating bourgeois guilt rather than genuinely posing a challenge to the causes of poverty has been extensively debated. Christopher Hitchens argued that 'the point is not the honest relief of suffering but the promulgation of a cult based on death and suffering and subjection.' The Gospel says – 'Blessed are the poor in spirit for theirs is the kingdom of heaven.' Poverty was something that managed to bring Mahatma Gandhi and Mother Teresa together. Both identified poor as the blessed and Gandhi's writings spoke of the dignity of poverty and inherent joy of poverty. Similarly, for Mother Teresa, poverty was beautiful and something to celebrate. Upon Mother Teresa's death, her successor Sister Nirmala noted that 'poverty will always exist. We want the poor to see poverty in the right way – to accept it and believe that the Lord will provide.' This philosophy does not encourage the poor to strive for substantive social change – it leads them to fatalism. If poverty is 'beautiful' and inevitable, there is really no point in identifying and combating the structures that produce poverty?

'Mother Teresa walked in step with Pope John Paul II who was not only opposed to abortion and women entering the priesthood, but who was not too keen on the radical edge of Liberation Theology. John Paul II invited the 'good nun' to the 1980 synod on marriage to denounce abortion and contraception and on February 5, 1994, at the National Prayer Breakfast in Washington DC, she announced extraordinarily that 'the greatest destroyer of peace today is abortion'! (National Catholic Reporter, September 19, 1997). Of Diana Spencer and Mother Teresa, Katha Pollitt rightly notes that they are 'flowers of hierarchical, feudal, essentially masculine institutions in which they had no structural power but whose authoritarian natures they obscured and prettified' (Katha Pollitt, 'Thoroughly Modern Di,' The Nation, September 29, 1997, page 9).

In certain instances, Mother Teresa seemed to be making exceptions to her own principles. During the referendum in Ireland to end the constitutional ban on divorce and remarriage in 1995, Mother Teresa traveled around the Emerald isle preaching against the feminists for whom this was an important battle (they won by a narrow 50.3 per cent against 49.7 per cent on November 24, 1995). At the same time, Charles and Diana Windsor spoke of moving from separation to divorce (on November 20, Diana gave an interview to BBC). Mother Teresa, in an interview to Ladies Home Journal, noted of that marriage that 'no one was happy' (Christopher Hitchens, *'Throne and Alter,' The Nation,* September 29, 1997, page 7).

For those in power, one has one set of principles and for those who are powerless, one has another.

'During the night of December 2-3, 1984, methyl isocyanate left the environs of a Union Carbide factory and poisoned thousands of people. The Bhopal massacre by Union Carbide was but the most flagrant example of a transnational corporation's disregard for human life at the expense of its own profit. In 1983, Union Carbide's sales came to $9 billion and its assets totalled $10 billion. Part of this profit came from a tendency to shirk any responsibility towards safety standards, not just in India, but also in their Virginia plant. After the disaster, Mother Teresa flew into Bhopal and, escorted in two government cars, she offered Bhopal's victims small aluminum medals of St. Mary. "This could have been an accident," she told the survivors, "its like a fire (that) could break out anywhere. That is why it is important to forgive. Forgiveness offers us a clean heart and people will be a hundred times better after it." John Paul II joined Mother Teresa with his analysis that Bhopal was a 'sad event' which resulted from 'man's efforts to make progress' [Tara Jones, *Corporate Killing: Bhopals Will Happen* (London: Free Association Books, 1988), page 32 and page 298]. There is something terrifying about these statements. Both are able to step away from what is widely recognized as a flagrant example of corporate greed' (Vijay Prashad Assistant Professor, International Studies, Trinity College, Hartford).

Even though her criticisms peaked during her lifetime, the deprived continued to find solace in Mother Teresa, disillusioned by the political gimmicks and bourgeois disinterest. She chose to live a sparton life – something that people could easily identify with. Her work was relevant to those who were struggling for their survival – the old, the poor, the sick and the unemployed. During January 1997, a documentary – entitled *Mother Teresa: Time for Change?* — critical of her working methods and accusing her of neglect, was shown on various European television channels. Mother Teresa never felt the need to protest against mudslinging, but there have been instances of serious litigations like the one with her one time close friend, the author, Dominique Lapierre over the script of a film based on her life. One of the well known letters of protest was written to Judge Lance protesting against what she perceived as the prosecution of her friend Charles Keating, widely acknowledged as the biggest fraudster in US history. After her death, her order continues with the litigious tradition – less than a year after her death it was involved in a court case with the Mother Teresa Memorial Committee, a Calcutta based organization.

An absolutely devastating criticism leveled against her by the German magazine, *Stern*, saying that her congregation is basically a religious order not worthy of being called a charitable foundation has not been contested by Missionaries of Charity. The article was called *'Mother Teresa, Where are your millions?'* and the research was conducted across three continents. These allegations definitely created turbulence for Mother Teresa but she always maintained that all this is being done for publicity. There have been instances when personal interviews were denied to journalists who had the reputation of being critical of Mother Teresa's activities. Some sections in the media believed that her image was carefully self-nurtured and sympathetic media persons always managed to get a hearing. It has been pointed out how she spent one full day talking to *'Hello'* magazine which published extensive interview of Mother Teresa and later her successor, sister Nirmala. Many people believed that Mother Teresa had been engaging herself in noble deeds and should not be cornered, but the critics maintain that more people were turned away than those who received help from her order and 'there was stupendous discrepancy between her work and her image; between her words and her deeds...It is our duty to stand up and protest when history is in danger of *being distorted.'* (Hitchens). It was Macaulay who said that the Roman Catholic Church deserved great credit for, and owed its longevity to its ability to handle and contain fanaticism but Mother Teresa's beatification, says Hitchens, 'is a surrender to showbiz and superstition.'

Following are the excerpts from the deposition, titled, *'Mother Teresa: Mother of All Myths'* submitted by Aroup Chatterjee before the Committee for beatification/canonization of Mother Teresa in February 1998:

'Being a lay person not versed in ecclesiastical procedures, I am not eminently suited to make a formal or technical deposition before the Committee. However, I have had a keen interest in Mother Teresa for the last few years and have researched her operations, perhaps more thoroughly than anyone else in the world. And, as somebody born, brought up and educated in Calcutta, I feel I am in a unique situation to offer evidence to the Committee. The Committee may summon me at any time to appear personally before it to offer evidence. I also put my audio-visual evidence at the disposal of the Committee should it want to consult them.'

'I believe that Mother Teresa had deliberately misled the world in her assertions about 'picking up' destitutes from the streets of Calcutta in order to bolster her own image and that of her faith. Her failure to provide vehicles (whilst continually claiming to do so) are even more significant because she had been donated a number of ambulance vehicles. These are used mainly (though not solely) as vans to ferry nuns, often to and from places of prayer. I believe that this constitutes an abuse of other people's trust in her... Mother Teresa once said, "If there are poor on the moon, we will go there." She said many times that she never refused anybody who needed help. In reality however, her order operated strict exclusion criteria in their selection of who to help and who not to. Mother Teresa's order did (does) not help anybody, no matter how poor or helpless, who had a family member of any kind—what they term a 'family case'. (That is one practice he doesn't like which I agree with. The family should take care of their own first. Too bad we don't do that here with welfare)...The Committee may also want to interview street children from around Mother House who were repeatedly reported to the police by Mother Teresa's nuns for 'pestering' foreigners who came to visit the 'living saint'. I have video interviews with such children, which the Committee may like to consult.'

'In her famous letter written in 1978 to the then Indian Prime Minister Morarji Desai in protest against the curbing of Christian missionary activities, Mother Teresa mentioned that she operated '102 centres' of natural family in Calcutta. The Committee should heed that such centres do not exist. The Committee should also note that in her Nobel Prize speech Mother Teresa had said that in six years in Calcutta there were '61,273 babies less' born because of her organization's natural family planning activities. There is no basis whatever for this statistic, and it was disingenuous of Mother Teresa to mention it in her Nobel Prize speech.'

Mother Teresa consistently maintained that she did not know anything about politics but she always voted in Indian elections and all her nuns also voted. What was more shocking and serious was her support of the State of Emergency in India (1995-1997). This phase saw the suspension of democratic rights and detention of many esteemed leaders without trials. Chatterjee concluded by saying that if sainthood is being conferred on her for being an exceptional Catholic, she deserves it but if one takes into consideration factors like honesty and integrity, then there will be a question mark.

Whichever way the argument proceeds, it is an undeniable fact that Mother Teresa was the most famous religious icon of the twentieth century. Gezim Alpion's book *Mother Teresa: Saint or Celebrity?* provides previously unknown facts about her personal life and makes an attempt to address the nature of her fame and devotion to faith. For Alpion, celebrity culture is a modern form of religion and

Mother Teresa was the ultimate religious celebrity of the modern era. While most other saints got recognition after their death, Mother Teresa's fame and sanctity took root in her lifetime. Alpion points out that the beatification of such a contemporary figure was as much a consequence of her growing stardom as it was of her devoted religious practice.

The missionaries have been zealous about conversions in India. Arun Shourie, in Missionaries in India, has pointed out that it costs $145 billion a year to operate global Christianity. According to Professor Gauri Vishwanathan in her book *Outside that Fold* 'religious conversion is probably one of the most unsettling political events in the life of any society.' Hindus often see the process of conversion to Christianity as a catalyst of change from Indian values to the western way of life. There was widespread criticism of mass conversions of children and the dying by Mother Teresa. We just have to turn the pages of history to realize how Hinduism has been under attack for thousands of years; first from Islam and then Christianity. Swami Vivekananda and Mahatma Gandhi both opposed this loss of identity. Most common evangelistic phrases like 'Hindus need to be saved from spiritual darkness,' church plantings, rich harvest of converts, idol worshippers and un-reached people' speak openly of 'spiritual conflict.' Sir John Woodroffe had predicted in his book, *Is India Civilized* page xlviii, that: ' In every way, the coming assault on Hindu civilization will be the greatest which it has ever had to endure in the whole course of its long history.'

Mahatma Gandhi called Christian missionaries, 'Vendors of Goods.' He said 'In Hindu households, the advent of a missionary has meant the disruption of the family coming in the wake of change of dress, manners, language, food and drink.' 'If I had power and could legislate, I should certainly stop all proselytizing.' 'I resent the overtures made to Harijans.' 'Stop all conversion; it is the deadliest poison that ever sapped the fountain of truth.' Poverty does not justify conversion. He also considered missionaries as 'a clear libel on Indian humanity.'

What followed in Mother Teresa's life is what Hitchens described as 'an argument not with a deceiver but with the deceived. If Mother Teresa is the adored object of many credulous and uncritical observers, then the blame is not hers, or hers alone. In the gradual manufacture of an illusion, the conjuror is only the instrument of the audience.'

Bibliography

- *No Greater Love* by Mother Teresa with a Foreword by Thomas Moore
- *A Simple Path* by Mother Teresa
- *Mother Teresa:* A Complete Authorized Biography by Kathryn Spink
- *The Missionary Position: Mother Teresa in Theory and Practice* by Christopher Hitchens
- BBC Reports
- *Time Magazine*
- *New York Times*
- *Such a Vision of the Street (Biography of Mother Teresa)* by Eileen Egan
- *Mother Teresa* An Authorized Biography by Navin Chawla
- *Everything Starts From Prayer* Mother Teresa's Meditations on Spiritual Life for People of All Faiths by Mother Teresa, selected and arranged by Anthony Stern, with a foreword by Larry Dossy
- *In the Heart of the World—Thoughts, Stories and Prayers* by Mother Teresa

○ *Do it Anyway—The Paradox-Finding Personal Meaning and Deep Happiness by Living the Pradoxical Commandments* by Kent M. Keith

○ *Mother Teresa's Secret Fire* by Joseph Langford

Pictures

www.literatepackrat.com/blogs/scrapebook/archives/in

www.edupe.ca/birchwood/peace/mt.htm

www.oilpaintingsgallery.com/gallery/oilpainting/i (cover page)

edition.cnn.com/WORLD/9709/13/teresa.service/index

www.rediff.com/news/1998/sep/04month4.htm